To Maro,
all the best wishes for
health and happiness —
Matilda Raffa Cuomo 2017

PROMINENT PEOPLE RECALL
THEIR MENTORS

THE

PERSON WHO
CHANGED MY
LIFE

EDITED BY MATILDA RAFFA CUOMO
FOREWORD BY HILLARY RODHAM CLINTON

RODALE.

© 1999, 2002, 2012 by Matilda Raffa Cuomo
Tony Bennett essay © 1999 by Tony Bennett
Nora Ephron essay © 2010 by Nora Ephron
Alan Schwartz essay © 2012 by Alan Schwartz

Rodale books may be purchased for business or promotional use or for special sales. For information, please write to:
Special Markets Department, Rodale Inc., 733 Third Avenue, New York, NY 10017

Printed in the United States of America
Printed with soy-based inks on 100% postconsumer waste paper.

Cover photo credits— Christiane Amanpour: Ida Mae Astute/American Broadcasting Companies, Inc.; Alec Baldwin: Brigitte Lacombe; Harry Belafonte: Pamela Belafonte; Tony Bennett: Paul Drinkwater/NBC; Andrea Bocelli: © 2008 by Luca Rossetti; Andrew Cuomo: Don Pollard; Christopher Cuomo: Heidi Gutman/American Broadcasting Companies, Inc.; Mario Cuomo: Don Pollard; Whoopi Goldberg: Timothy White; Mehmet Oz: Robert Trachtenberg, Sony Pictures Television; Diane Sawyer: Ida Mae Astute/American Broadcasting Companies, Inc.; Fareed Zakaria: Justin Larose

Additional jacket photo credits for hardcover edition—Alan Alda: courtesy of Alan Alda; Joy Behar: courtesy of CNN; Michael Bloomberg: Spencer Tucker; Kenneth Cole: Richard Phibbs; Nora Ephron: Ilona Lieberman; Charles Grodin: Videler Photography; Marcia Gay Harden: Thaddeus Harden; Rosie O'Donnell: Dan Fineman; Robin Roberts: Donna Svennevik/American Broadcasting Companies, Inc.; Martin Sheen: Courtesy of Martin Sheen

Book design by Christopher Rhoads

Library of Congress Cataloging-in-Publication Data

The person who changed my life : prominent people recall their mentors / edited by Matilda Raffa Cuomo.
     p.   cm.
Updated ed. of: The person who changed my life : prominent Americans recall their mentors. c1999.
    ISBN 978–1–60529–122–2 paperback
    ISBN 978–1–60961–335–X hardcover
    ISBN 978–1–60961–903–9 hardcover (2nd Edition)
    1. Self-actualization (Psychology) 2. Motivation (Psychology) 3. Mentoring.
I. Cuomo, Matilda.
BF637.S4P445 2011
371.102—dc22
                                        2010047795

Distributed to the trade by Macmillan
   4 6 8 10 9 7 5   paperback
2 4 6 8 10 9 7 5 3 1 hardcover (2nd Edition)

We inspire and enable people to improve their lives and the world around them.
www.rodalebooks.com

To my husband, Mario, and our children and grandchildren.
May you always have faith, hope, and love.
May your light shine all the days of your lives.

"Kids don't need you to be superman. They just need you to be there. They need you to be someone they can count on. It's about building that trust. It's about providing comfort and stability in a world that often lacks both. And it's about showing young people that the world is filled with opportunities, and then helping them seize those opportunities."

—First Lady Michelle Obama,
National Mentoring Summit, January 2011

CONTENTS

ACKNOWLEDGMENTS

I would like to acknowledge Maria Rodale for recognizing the importance of mentoring for at-risk youth in America and publishing this special edition of *The Person Who Changed My Life*. I am grateful for the leadership of Rodale publisher Karen Rinaldi, who believed in this project and contributed her strategic and creative vision. We owe special thanks to our patient and diligent editor, Gena Smith, who coordinated the book design and content. Thanks to Rodale's philanthropic generosity, we will be able to gain resources through the sale of this book to further mentoring services for children in need.

My special appreciation for the efforts of Mentoring USA executive director Stephen Powell and the team who worked on the collection of essays, including Karen Salerno, Wendy Gerber, and our dear friend and longtime associate, Kristin Hoppmann Mangler. I am deeply grateful to my daughter, Maria Cuomo Cole, for her tremendous contribution of time and management directing this project and supervising Mentoring USA under the auspices of the agency she leads with such devotion, HELP USA. My gratitude to all the extraordinary contributors for sharing their meaningful stories of the personal mentors who helped change their lives.

FOREWORD
BY HILLARY
RODHAM CLINTON

I first met Matilda Raffa Cuomo when our husbands served as governors. I remember how much I immediately liked her and how passionately she talked about the importance of mentoring in the lives of our young people. She explained her efforts in New York to launch the nation's first statewide, one-to-one mentoring program. Over the years, at events at the White House or in New York, Matilda and I have continued our conversations about what mentoring has meant in our own lives and our common commitment to open up those same opportunities to all children.

I am grateful to so many people—teachers, coaches, neighbors—who encouraged, supported, and challenged me while I was growing up. I will always be thankful to Rev. Donald James, my church's youth minister in Park Ridge, Illinois, who did so much to open a wider world to me and my friends. He arranged for our church youth group to worship and participate in service projects together with black and Hispanic teenagers in Chicago. He exposed us to modern art and poetry, from Picasso to e. e. cummings, long before school did. And in 1961 he took a group of us to hear Dr. Martin Luther King Jr. speak. As I listened to Dr. King's powerful words about nonviolence and the right of all Americans to live in dignity, I knew my world would never be the same.

Adults can have mentors, too. I had one after I met Marian Wright Edelman during my first year of Yale Law School. Marian, a civil rights lawyer and children's advocate, inspired my own commitment to justice. Marian also knows about mentoring. As she writes about growing up in South Carolina before the civil rights era, she describes how she and her sisters "were wrapped up and rocked in the cradle of faith, song, prayer, ritual, and worship, which immunized our spirits against some of the meanness and unfairness of our segregated South." I have felt that cloak of protection working in my own life. And I have seen how parents, church leaders, teachers, and other caring adults have sustained and supported young people in times of sorrow, pain, or confusion.

This book is filled with stories of people who were lucky enough to be embraced by that same loving web of relationships, and who, as a result, found the strength and direction to overcome barriers to success and freedom. Their stories underscore what we know by experience to be true—that even one caring adult in the life of a young person can make all the difference in the world, opening up opportunities that may have seemed unimaginable.

Every child needs a champion. Yet, for too many of America's children today, there are no champions; there are no mentors. Some young people may need tutoring help in school so they can feel the satisfaction of reading a good book and being promoted to the next class. Others may need coaching in a sport so they can experience what it is like to be engaged in team effort. Many children thrive when they are given the opportunity to contribute, whether in building a home for a homeless person or tutoring a young sibling or classmate. Every young person needs someone to say, "I believe in you."

I've seen the power of mentoring firsthand. For example, I have visited the Harriet Tubman School in Harlem, New York, where parents and members of the community were coming together to create after-school programs that are currently boosting students' grades and self-confidence. I have seen the excitement in the eyes of young inner-city children in Washington, DC, as they looked forward to meeting with volunteers from AmeriCorps, who were helping them with their reading skills. And I have seen what can happen when artists, poets, and musicians unleash the creative imaginations of young people, turning a dreary classroom into a set for a play or a place to explore the wonders of a flute or a paintbrush.

Mentoring. Tutoring. After-school programs. There are many opportunities for caring, responsible adults to become involved in the lives of our children. At a time when there seems to be so little that people agree on, this is one mission worthy of bipartisan, broad-based support. It is not only the right thing to do, it is the smart thing to do. We know from countless studies that there are direct links between mentoring and tutoring programs and higher academic achievement, lower dropout rates, fewer teen pregnancies, and safer communities.

I hope this book will inspire more people to become involved in the life of a young person, because we all have a critical role to play. I also hope it will persuade governors and legislators to invest more of their budgets in mentoring and other support programs for our young people. I was pleased that my husband, while president, signed into law the GEAR UP program, which has encouraged middle schoolers in some of our poorest neighborhoods to begin thinking about going to college and has recruited mentors to help them make that dream a reality. The government clearly has a role to play. But in the end, it is up to each and every one of us to become involved in a child's life.

There are many successful mentoring programs across the country that are making a difference in the lives of young people, thanks to leaders like Matilda Cuomo. Whether people enlist in a local mentoring program, informally start helping a child, or participate in national efforts like Mentoring USA, "I Have a Dream" programs, or the Boys & Girls Clubs of America, the result is the same. By giving one-to-one attention to a troubled child, offering hope where there is only despair, or opening doors that were once shut, we can change lives. These are some of the best investments we can make to ensure that children not only survive but thrive in today's world.

For America to succeed in the twenty-first century everyone deserves a good education, and everyone should have the opportunity to go to college. We cannot afford to let only the privileged have those chances and dream those dreams. As a nation we must ensure that all children, regardless of their race, neighborhood, or family income, have the opportunity to fulfill their God-given potential and the skills they need to grow and flourish. Let us teach our children that they can go as far as their dreams and abilities will take them. Let us stand beside them, believe in them, and help guide them, until they get there.

—Hillary Rodham Clinton

INTRODUCTION

Today mentoring is recognized as one of our most effective social programs, one which encourages and facilitates the education and the self-confidence of the mentee. At a mentoring summit in January 2011, President Obama, referring to the heightened need for volunteers to mentor at-risk children, issued a call to action: "Academic achievement and social success through mentoring." I heartily endorse the president's initiative. He has given us a great national challenge—we want to connect mentors with young people in one hundred and seventy communities that comprise the two thousand lowest-performing schools in the United States. This third edition of *The Person Who Changed My Life* provides further evidence of the importance and effectiveness of mentoring, especially after a serious economic recession left us with a large increase in the number of troubled families and at-risk children in need of help. The evidence comes in the form of testimony from many more prominent Americans recalling their mentors and a brief review of their memorable experiences.

Mentoring USA started in 1983 at the outset of my husband Mario's twelve years as governor of New York State. The state was confronted with an economic recession, a large budget deficit, and a widely available, inexpensive new drug called crack. When my husband shared with me the alarming school dropout rate in New York State, we agreed on the necessity of finding an effective strategy to encourage children to stay in school and continue their education.

Mario asked for ideas about how to ameliorate this problem, and I told him that all my experiences as a child, a teacher, and a mother

seemed to point to one solution: match every at-risk child with a caring, trained volunteer adult—a mentor. He agreed, and together we
gathered a statewide, nonpartisan committee of volunteers with exper-
tise in all the relevant areas of child development. They were called
upon to develop a plan of action, which they did with enthusiasm and
efficiency. Mentoring was to be one of the state's major programs,
reaching children at an early age before destructive habits became too
complex to address. It was also decided that mentoring on a one-to-
one basis would ensure the best results.

In 1987, the New York State Mentoring Program was established
as the first statewide, school-based, one-to-one volunteer mentoring
program in the country, serving children from kindergarten through
eighth grade. At the time, the value of mentoring children was not as
well known and understood as it is today, so our first mission utilizing
Greek methology was to introduce the mentoring concept to important community leaders around the state. After the first several
months, hundreds of chief executive officers, school administrators,
teachers, politicians, and neighborhood activists were telling other
potential volunteers about the adventures of Odysseus in the Trojan
War and how he left his beloved son Telemachus in the care of Mentor,
his trusted counselor and loyal friend. Today the mentoring concept is
popular all over America.

The New York State Mentoring Program proved to be a successful
model. It emphasizes a team approach that links parents, teachers, and
mentors as essential partners in every child's success. My belief is that
the well-being of every child depends on three pillars of support: the
home, the school, and the community. When one of these supports is
missing, dysfunctional, or inadequate, the child suffers. In too many
cases, the child performs poorly in school, makes bad choices, or does
not achieve his or her potential. The evidence is all around us.

Too many children in America are struggling to find their way
through the perils of drugs, alcohol, and dangerous permissiveness

without good adult role models. Without anyone to turn to for guidance, they would have very little hope for the future. Our youth depend on school administrators or their teachers to provide a positive role model.

I was luckier than many of these children, and, like many of our mentors, I wanted to share some of my good fortune with today's troubled young people. Like many first-generation Americans growing up in the 1940s, I missed kindergarten and began school in the first grade, as required by law. At the time, there was little interaction between families and schools, and little tolerance for non-English-speaking immigrants, like my parents. I remember the pain of witnessing my mother's embarrassment when the principal brusquely ordered us to leave school because my mother was unable to fill out the enrollment forms for kindergarten. As we walked home she squeezed my hand, and I watched her eyes fill with tears of embarrassment and frustration. This memory has always reminded me of the resilience, courage, and love it took for her to raise five children. Mentors try to bring some of these qualities to those they mentor.

When I attended P.S. 137 in Brooklyn, I was shy and insecure, unwilling to speak or assert myself in class. The first person to single me out for the encouragement I needed was Mrs. Kulyer, my fourth-grade teacher. She took the time to talk to me, draw me out, and share my thoughts about what I might do when I grew up. She was my first mentor beyond my parents. When Mrs. Kulyer told me I would make a great teacher, a whole world opened up. I rushed home to tell my parents the good news, and I never forgot her advice and encouragement. Years later, I was teaching second grade in a public school in Elmont, Long Island.

My good fortune in being befriended by my fourth-grade teacher and other mentoring role models taught me that the reassurance of a devoted parent might not be enough for a child, especially one passing through the turbulence of preadolescence. Reflecting on my own years as a parent of five children, it is clear to me now that if I had been a single parent struggling to raise a family and earn a living, the need for outside support would have been essential. And the school would have been a good place to find that support.

For that reason, the New York State Mentoring Program found strong allies in school principals and teachers. The instant success of the program was proof that placing children first has an impact on all aspects of family and community life. We learned that children, matched one-to-one with responsible volunteer mentors, demonstrated more confidence and a greater interest in school, increasing their chances of finishing high school and moving on to higher education or productive, fulfilling jobs. Between 1987 and 1995, we served ten thousand children from Buffalo to Long Island through the prodigious efforts of thousands of volunteers from all walks of life—corporations, government, and the community.

In 1995, after my husband left public service, the New York State Mentoring Program was discontinued by the new state administration. I was saddened by the development, but with my family's encouragement, I established Mentoring USA as a private, nonprofit organization with initial financial support from Mr. Howard Maier and Mr. Martin Silverman, two highly intelligent and generous New York businessmen.

In 1986, my son Andrew, as a young lawyer, founded HELP USA, a pro bono program to help homeless adults and children in need become and remain self-reliant through the development of quality housing with on-site, comprehensive support services, including job training and placement programs. HELP USA continues today to enable its residents to become independent and productive citizens. It breaks the cycle of dependency by addressing its underlying causes in a way that respects the dignity of those we serve by helping them to help themselves.

My daughter, Maria Cuomo Cole, has been chairperson of HELP USA since 1993, when Andrew began serving in Washington as assistant secretary to the Department of Housing and Urban Development. Under her leadership, HELP USA has become the nation's largest builder, developer, and operator of transitional and permanent low-income housing, with comprehensive, on-site human services for the homeless. It was clear from experience that the children in the HELP USA facilities would benefit from the caring relationship that Mentoring USA could provide.

Since 1996, Mentoring USA continues the model and mission of the original New York State Mentoring Program and has expanded to become national, and even international (Mentoring USA/Italia and Mentoring USA España). We've learned that both the problems children face and the efficacy of mentoring in solving these problems are truly universal. Indeed, I am often reminded of one of my father's favorite expressions, "*Tutto il mondo é paese*"—"all the world is one."

The Mentoring USA Program has continued its original BRAVE (Bias Related Anti-Violence Education) training program, which teaches children to live without hate and bullying via positive adult mentors. The objectives of the BRAVE program include fostering a greater awareness and respect for the diversity of people and reaffirming knowledge and respect for one's own culture and heritage in order to appreciate and respect the culture and heritage of others. The goal of BRAVE is to improve measurably a child's chance of living a more harmonious, peaceful, and productive life through specialized mentor trainings with resources and interactive activities on tolerance to prevent bullying. In light of all the hate crimes recently committed in New York City, it should also be noted that Mentoring USA operates a special program site for teens in the LGBTQ (lesbian, gay, bisexual, transgender, and questioning) community in an effort to provide a safe space for open expression and a celebration of diversity for the teenagers and adults in this program.

Mentoring USA's Healthy Lifestyle and Self Esteem initiative aims to have the mentor serve as a model for healthy lifestyle choices and to help increase the mentees self-confidence. According to the Centers for Disease Control and Prevention, one in three US children are overweight while 15 percent are obese. Knowing the impact of poor food choices and physical inactivity, Mentoring USA's Healthy Lifestyle and Self-Esteem initiative provides interactive activities to increase a child's knowledge about nutrition, diet, physical activity, and the importance of sustainable health habits. This initiative is supported through partnerships with the Cornell Cooperative Extension, Dr. Mehmet Oz's HealthCorps, the United States Tennis Association, and Nike.

Mentoring USA's Foster Care program is uniquely designed to provide structured, one-to-one mentoring for youth in foster care throughout New York City. These specialized program sites follow the same important guidelines as the original Mentoring USA General Programs do, all while expanding service to youth up to twenty-one years of age. When foster care children turn twenty-one and "age out" of the system, they are presented with a whole new set of challenges, many of which their mentors can help them overcome. Mentoring USA's Foster Care program passionately aims to provide these youth with someone who cares, in order to develop a long-term relationship increasing the likelihood of future success. Additionally, Mentoring USA has a focus on capacity building and training for mentors and mentees involved in foster care mentoring with two new initiatives—Foster Care Mentoring Institute and Youth Financial Empowerment.

The Foster Care Mentoring Institute has strengthened and expanded mentoring programs for youth in foster care by providing comprehensive, specialized trainings. A partnership was developed with Mentoring USA, NYC Children's Services, the New York Junior League, and Changing the World One Child at a Time. The Foster Care Mentoring Institute's specialized trainings have included the following topics: "Understanding Your Mentee's Emotional/Behavioral Issues," "Understanding the Child Welfare System," "The Role of a Mentor in

Foster Care Mentoring," and "Active Listening, Teen Sexuality, and Understanding Separation and Loss Issues for Foster Care Youth."

The Youth Financial Empowerment (YFE) initiative is a financial education and savings program that teaches children in foster care sound money management skills and helps them build assets for their future. Using a special account called an Individual Development Account, foster care youth save up to $1,000 and YFE matches it with $2,000. The foster care youth are paired with a trained/screened Mentoring USA mentor after the youth complete eight sessions of financial literacy training. The organizational partners involved in this initiative include NYC Children's Services, Citibank, New Yorkers for Children, and the United Way.

The general Financial Literacy initiative of Mentoring USA teaches children the fundamentals of how to manage, budget, save, spend, and invest money. Supported by alliances including the NASDAQ OMX Educational Foundation, Operation Hope, Citi, and NYU Stern, the goal of Financial Literacy is to measurably improve a child's chance of realizing financial independence. Mentors and mentees utilize the Citigroup Financial Education Curriculum, Mentoring USA financial literacy activities with guest speakers and facilitators.

In Newark, New Jersey, Mentoring USA works with Mayor Cory Booker's senior staff that mentors children at the Eighteenth Avenue School, as well as a faith-based mentoring partnership with Metropolitan Baptist Church and partnerships with Communities in Schools and Greater Newark CARES. New programs have also been launched in Houston through the Harris County Department of Education; in Las Vegas through a technical assistance partnership with Susan Taylor's National CARES Mentoring Movement; in Los Angeles through LA's BEST After School Program; in Illinois and Maryland through Bloomingdale's and Polished Pebbles Inc.; and with NASDAQ OMX, Verizon, NYC Service, 100 Black Men and FFAWN in New York.

Bloomingdale's alone has provided over one hundred and fifty employees to serve as mentors in four US markets. Their annual "Fashionable Fundraiser," benefitting Mentoring USA, provides an opportunity for program expansion, employee participation, and mentoring advocacy. Macy's Inc., equally committed to Mentoring USA's program expansion, has also engaged their employees in supporting mentoring expansion and academic achievement via their "Partners in Time" effort.

Today, Mentoring USA functions as a school- and site-based mentoring program. Mentoring USA partners with the faith-based community, public and charter schools, the government, housing facilities, community centers, foster care agencies, and the private sector to form a unified team to provide supervised, site-based, one-to-one mentoring, matching youth between the ages of seven and twenty-one with caring, trained adult mentors. Our volunteer mentors are carefully screened and trained. They make a commitment to mentor a child one-to-one, four hours a week, for a full year. Many mentors continue with the same child for an average of three to five years.

Nationally and locally, Mentoring USA currently serves communities via technical assistance and program management in New York City; Newark, New Jersey; Houston; Denver; Las Vegas; Chicago; Los Angeles; Syracuse, New York; Atlanta; Philadelphia; and Louisville.

Internationally, Mentoring USA/Italia was created in 1998 to address the high school dropout rate, which is the cause of social vices such as microcriminality, bullying, violence, and drug addiction in Italy. Mentoring USA has expanded in other regions including Spain.

Over a decade ago, I was brainstorming with my staff and family about creative outreach and strategies to promote mentoring. My daughter, Madeline, suggested a book project—a compilation of personal stories about influential mentors written by outstanding individuals from all walks of life, including the worlds of politics, entertainment, business, and the arts. I thought this would be a perfect way to persuade potential volunteers that their efforts to become mentors really do make a difference in the lives of our youth. The process proved to be an invaluable work experience—much more rewarding than I could ever have imagined.

The men and women whose stories we have included in this third edition offer more wonderful proof of the effectiveness of mentoring. These individuals have risen to the top of their fields, distinguishing themselves in great and small ways. Walter Cronkite once said that no one does anything in life on his own, that there are always caring people who shape our lives and our careers, whose influence stays with us for the rest of our lives. The essays in this edition are a testimony to this truth, and a tribute to all the people who have helped shape the lives of children. We are grateful to all the extraordinary people who took the time and made the effort to share their mentors with us.

It is clear that the mentors brought to life in these essays have not been forgotten, and they are, in every sense of the word, true heroes and heroines. It is my fervent hope that the stories of these admired and successful men and women will inspire many others to make similar investments in the future of our children. Mentoring is a lifetime investment in a child; children will always remember their mentors with joy and gratitude, and mentors themselves will also have a fulfilling memory to cherish.

—*Matilda Raffa Cuomo*

ALAN ALDA
MAKE DISTINCTIONS

I've had many mentors—teachers, fellow actors, and writers—but there's really only one I couldn't have done without.

I needed to have someone who was there when I made big decisions. And even more, the small ones—because even if they're only a fraction of a degree off, small decisions can add up and move you in a direction you never really wanted to take.

I didn't need a mentor who would pronounce a few words to the wise and then take off for an early dinner. I needed someone at my elbow, working on the deeper stuff.

It wasn't enough to be taught a skill or guided toward a career. From the time I was a boy, standing in the wings watching performers, I knew what my career would be, and I began at an early age to learn the skills of the trade. In fact, that was my problem: I grew up on the stage and I tended to think of other people as an audience. I knew how to make sure they were there for me, but I didn't understand yet how I could also be there for them. I needed to exit the stage door and get out onto the street.

It would take luck to find someone who could open that door. And I was lucky.

While I was still young, my mentor helped me change my thinking. "Make distinctions," she'd say. I didn't understand what she meant at first, but after a while I realized that other people's behavior didn't always need an all-or-nothing response. I learned to

1

distinguish the good qualities in a person from the not so good and cherish the good.

Years later, after that thought had sunk in, I put it this way to my daughter as she graduated from college: "A peach is not its fuzz, a toad is not its warts, a person is not his or her crankiness. If we can make distinctions, we can be tolerant, and we can get to the heart of our problems instead of wrestling endlessly with their gross exteriors." I even saw that it went further than that. "Once you make a habit of making distinctions," I told her, "you'll begin challenging your own assumptions. Your assumptions are your windows on the world. Scrub them off every once in a while or the light won't come in." None of this would ever have occurred to me if not for the most important mentor in my life.

I was lucky to find someone I could trust enough to let in close. Someone who could accept me as I was and yet see more in me than I knew was there and lead me gently down the long road toward compassion.

When you find someone as profoundly helpful as that, you want to hang on to that person for as long as you can. And I did.

I married her.

CHRISTIANE AMANPOUR
STAYING THE COURSE

Every time you fall, you pick yourself up, dust yourself off,
and keep going.

Growing up in Iran, I attended a riding school run by a former Iranian army cavalry officer who used the very European method of teaching. This became my sport, as well as racing horses, which I did until I outgrew the jockey limit of height and weight.

Several times a week, beginning when I was just five years old, I would be put on a large horse, not a small pony, which immediately set the bar high for what I was expected to do, how I was expected to deal with a big challenge.

The very act of accommodating another living being, whether human or animal, provides an unforgiving set of demands. I knew I couldn't treat the horse like a beast of burden. In order to get the best performance, my instructor taught me that I had to be kind to the horse and show a sense of shared endeavor, while also always showing the horse who was boss, not through kicking, whipping, or yanking the bit in his mouth, but by developing a more subtle mix of compassion and control.

I used to fall off the horse regularly, but there was no question of walking away or giving in to fear or stopping the exercise midway.

My instructor would walk over, pat my cheek, and lift me straight back on. Even though at the time I probably didn't understand courage, it was a very early lesson in staying the course. Every time you fall, you pick yourself up, dust yourself off, and keep going.

As it turned out, the lessons I learned riding formed a strong foundation for the extreme profession of living and working in war zones and other disasters that I've taken on. But I was also well equipped with all that I learned from my mother and father. My father is Muslim and Iranian; my mother is Catholic and English; and by their example, I learned about tolerance and that people and nations can, and must, coexist.

My career is based on reporting the divisions between civilizations, religions, and ethnicities. Our strength lies not in reinforcing what separates us but in overcoming diversity and building on it as a source of strength.

DAVE ANNABLE
FULFILLING MY DREAM

Believe it or not, it's my younger sister who most influenced my life. I've learned more from her than any other person in my life. My parents were instrumental, of course, and the best friends I could have. However, when I reflect back on who I am and what I've become, clearly I couldn't have done it without my sister, Rebecca.

We're pretty close in age, just about two years apart. High school was a very rough time for me. Rebecca was definitely the cool one—and I was not. I was on special meds that contained steroids for my asthma, and they caused me to gain weight, which affected my confidence. Rebecca was beautiful. She was voted not only most beautiful girl in the class but class president.

Yet, she didn't get there by being the "mean girl" in the most popular clique. She was everyone's best friend. She was my best friend. She valued things in people that were actually important, and she made me learn to do the same.

When I was younger, I wanted to have a career in film and television. I was still talking about it when I got to college, even though I had very little acting experience.

One day Rebecca called to say she found an advertisement in our small town newspaper. The ad called for models and actors to come to the Holiday Inn to meet real agents. I was so scared and nervous but agreed only if she would come with me. She did and I made my first callback, and then another, and ultimately landed an agent in

New York City. I completed five or six national commercials in that first year. From then on my confidence and career continued to grow.

Rebecca was the one who actually motivated me to be an actor. She taught me if you want to do something, you have to take action. Success cannot be achieved if you never take that first step. Thanks to Rebecca, I am now fulfilling my dream. Thanks, Beck.

EDWARD ASNER

A SOLID FOUNDATION MAKES EVERYTHING POSSIBLE

Two men who served in World War II before returning to careers in the Kansas City public schools were my mentors: my high school football coach, Ed Ellis, and my journalism teacher, George Corporon.

Corporon, who had served as a battlefield historian, came back looking frail, as if he had been witness to a great many things. He never burdened us with them but instilled in us an awe and respect for journalism as it should be. I was the first guy he let edit the paper while playing football. He was probably the most intellectual of my then-teachers, which intrigued me, and he stimulated me to know more of the world and the finer things in it.

One of the most significant exchanges I had with Coach Ellis happened before I actually played for him. I would see him around my best friend's house fairly often, because he and my friend's father, the swim coach, were great pals. He was a charming and wonderful man with a great spirit and the ability to fill those around him with it. This particular afternoon I was ranting and raving about the striking coal miners, having been led to believe by the Republican newspapers that punitive measures should be taken. Coach Ellis simply and totally rebuked me: "Well, Ed. You can't take away a man's right to strike."

I was so shocked by his answer, which flew in the face of prevailing opinion in my hometown, that it kept me in awe of him forever after and helped me to become a union man.

Both George Corporon and Coach Ellis showed me what quality and higher stature should look like and what I should aspire to. They helped inculcate in me a deep sense of fairness, by their words and the even more impressive example of their own behavior, which continues to inform every sphere of my life, from the political to the personal to the professional. I grew up in Kansas City as the youngest of a large clan. To have adults in my life who didn't see me as the baby of the family but as an individual—a knowledgeable and capable individual— was very good for me.

The major turning points in my life—discovering a passion for acting in my first college production, landing the part of Lou Grant, being elected president of the Screen Actors Guild, among others— didn't, of course, happen out of the blue. They were each just one of many possible consequences of a whole string of earlier events, decisions, and happy accidents.

So, no, Coach Ellis never suggested I give up football for the school play. But he and George Corporon and all the other good people I was lucky enough to have in my early life did help make me into someone with the self-knowledge and self-confidence to pursue the things that really mattered to me. They gave me the solid foundation that made everything possible. They had a real impact, not just on my life, but on the lives of so many young people. And all with very little noise. Their influence made me realize that there's too much glory when I do something (or sometimes opprobrium, but mostly glory).

It's people like them, whose contributions aren't written up in the press or recognized with awards and applause, who really knock my socks off: the people who struggle as labor organizers; nurses who go far beyond the call of duty; caring teachers who often spend their own money so their kids can go further; social workers, who perform one of the roughest jobs in the world, a job that eats you up, but they constantly find ways to help the less fortunate; people who run soup kitchens and missions; and, above all, the anonymous donors of this world.

ALEC BALDWIN

COURAGE IS NECESSARY FOR CREATIVITY TO THRIVE

Elaine Aiken was my acting coach and friend for nearly twenty years before she died of cancer in 1998. I first met Elaine at the Lee Strasberg Theatre Institute, where she taught acting classes. Although not a student of hers back in 1979, I began studying with her privately a few years after I left school. Elaine was an intelligent, fiercely opinionated, loving, and confident woman, someone who took acting quite seriously, but not so much as to be paralyzed by its inherent self-consciousness and self-delusions.

Acting is an art form that, above all, requires courage, and Elaine Aiken instilled in her students the valuable lesson that renewal of that courage is essential for creativity to thrive. She asked her students to consider their limitations, or at least their perceived limitations, and to wonder if they might overcome them with simple and focused effort.

When I performed in *A Streetcar Named Desire* on Broadway, there was a detached sexuality and languid masculinity in the character of Stanley Kowalski that we both agreed was a direction I should go. Now, I don't know how sexually cool and languidly masculine I appeared, but Elaine's work with me on that character, on the simple truth that Stanley had doubts about who he was and what he wanted in this world, led me to one of the most pleasurable experiences of my career.

Elaine Aiken gave me the greatest gifts one can give to a friend: love and support. And she gave me the greatest gifts that a teacher can give to a student: confidence and passion. Without my friendship with Elaine, I do not believe that I would have enjoyed my work as much as I have these past thirty years.

WILLIAM BALDWIN

A COACH FOR ALL SEASONS

My father, Alec, was the greatest mentor and inspiration in my life. He influenced the lives of many people in our community as a teacher and coach at Massapequa High School on Long Island for thirty-two years. He was also involved with many extra-curricular programs like Cub Scouts, Little League, and summer recreation programs. My father was, indeed, a pillar of our community. There were not many individuals or families whose lives were not influenced by or who had not benefitted from my father's kindness, devotion, and wisdom. I was extremely lucky during my childhood, because while my father did not enjoy the luxuries of material wealth, there was no shortage of discipline, advice, and love.

Aside from my parents, Al and Cathy Bevilacqua were, without question, the greatest influences in my life. Their home was around the corner from ours. I vividly remember sitting at their kitchen table during many hot, muggy summer evenings talking with Mrs. Bevilacqua. We would have many philosophical and inspirational discussions about topics ranging from family and marriage to education and spirituality. She was a tremendous influence and inspiration to me during childhood. She was wise, spiritual, and kind. She taught me to challenge myself both intellectually and culturally. She helped me to grow and evolve as a human being. She taught me to stay motivated, to be productive, to be of service, and to persevere. She continuously communicated these themes to me throughout my childhood.

Her husband, Al, is a legendary figure in the sport of wrestling. He is one of the most influential, respected, and celebrated coaches in the history of the sport. Coaching was never only about winning for him. It was about discipline, work ethic, mental toughness, and learning. It was about instilling values and providing tools for young people to take with them and utilize for the rest of their lives. These tools would help create productive, responsible young adults. They influence my life today—how I raise my own children, how I make decisions regarding my career. They are at the core of my existence, and I have the sport of wrestling and, more specifically, Al Bevilacqua to thank for it. For this, I am forever indebted to him.

Hopefully, everyone has a teacher from their childhood who stands out. One who made an indelible impression. One who inspired them and helped shape their life.

Maria Bartiromo
Mama's Girl

I'm really a mama's girl. Even though she was not a financial whiz, my mom instilled in me at a very young age the importance of saving and investing. Throughout my childhood, I can remember hearing and seeing constant reminders of hard work, saving, and financial independence.

I remember, for example, hearing the ice cream truck on my block in Brooklyn and springing into action. I would ask my mother if I could have an ice cream cone and she would always say, "Sure, but how are you going to pay for it?" I started to collect change in a jar, and I would then check my jar to see if I had enough pennies, nickels, or quarters to get what I wanted.

It would have been easy enough for my mother to hand me, or my sister and brother, the money to buy what we needed (within reason, of course). Instead she taught us that if you want something, you have to save for it. I remember her working so hard to put money in Christmas Clubs in the bank, which was a basic savings account. My mom would open the account in January and add to it every month. Every Christmas, she would then give it to my brother, sister, and me as a gift to buy presents for everyone. Even more important was watching her save money every month; it taught me the same lesson over and over again. As a result, even as a little girl I was watching and learning by her example.

My mother has always been a very hard worker, but even beyond her there is a long history of a strong work ethic in my family. A genealogist recently sent me a picture of the *Rex*, the ship that my grandfather sailed on from Italy to Ellis Island in 1919. It made me so proud. Imagine the courage it must have taken to leave his life as a bricklayer and start a whole new story here in America. He built a restaurant in Brooklyn and named it the Rex Manor after the ship he sailed on. The Rex Manor was passed down to my father, who eventually gave me my first job as the coat check girl. For me, this began a lifetime of hard work. And I cherish my grandfather and parents every day for making this work ethic possible for me.

I never had a grand plan to go into financial news, but there's no question in my mind that my upbringing planted the seeds of my career.

I'm not saying there weren't others who supported me along the way, mentors like Jack Welch, Jeff Immelt, Diane Sawyer, and Dick Grasso, who as head of the New York Stock Exchange made it possible for me to become the first journalist—man or woman—to report live from the floor of the New York Stock Exchange. This was during what would become the longest bull market in history. When I first got down there, it was more or less a "men's club," and some of them did not want me on their turf. Not only was I a woman, but a reporter with a camera.

I was just a few weeks into the job when I heard that Jack Welch, then chairman and CEO of GE, was coming down to the floor. As I was a reporter at CNBC, he was my big boss, and I thought, "How perfect; I am the representative of the company at the NYSE and I can at least show him the post and specialist" (the specialist is the point person for bringing buyers and sellers together).

A couple of days before Mr. Welch was scheduled to come in, I noticed that the GE post didn't look too busy. I started walking in that direction to speak with the person who oversaw all of the stock trading in GE and there were about twenty-five guys within earshot. One of the traders, however, did not want me anywhere near the post. I was mortified when this older man began yelling, "This is not your business. You will not come here. You will not ask questions— *run along!*" Although I had knots in my stomach, I calmly said, "Do not speak to me that way"—and walked away!

I eventually learned this man was actually on the board of the NYSE. I knew that he, and others like him, were not going to go away. For five years, I would take the most inconvenient routes just to avoid running into him and having to hear his belittling comments. It was unbelievable how tough he made it for me. But I kept coming back and told myself, "I'm going to study, and study again, and these guys won't have anything on me." By the way, there were also many, many people at the NYSE who welcomed me and supported me greatly.

Of course, a few individuals may not have wanted me there, but a hundred million Americans were investing and wanted to see the action. I was happy to be part of something new—giving the public access to the trading floor. It was a demystification of the process.

My mother taught me that it takes courage to have confidence— and because I had followed her advice, I developed the confidence that I knew my stuff. I learned from my mother that nothing comes easy, there are no shortcuts, and if you want it, the only way to get it is through hard work.

JOY BEHAR

AUNT SADIE SAYS TAKE RISKS

I had no real desire to try to be a professional actor or comedian. I was too shy and too scared. So I continued with my education, eventually got my master's degree in teaching, and became a teacher. I taught all through my twenties, but inside I wanted to do something different. I really wanted to act; I wanted to try comedy. Finally, in my early thirties, I told myself that I would do it, and I did.

My Aunt Sadie always encouraged me to take risks. There were times when my mom would ask how much longer I was going to "try this comedy thing." In the routine I would say, "One more year," and my mom would reply, "Six more months."

Luckily for me, Aunt Sadie would intervene on my behalf. "You take as long as you need to," she would say. And I did. I took her intervention as a sign of her faith in me; she really believed in me and what I was striving for. My mother believed in me, too, but she was more nervous about it.

Others who gave me support were female therapists. Luckily for me, I have had three amazing female therapists. Some people are embarrassed to admit that they're in therapy. Not me! These women really had a profound influence on my life. They helped me through some difficult times. I know of people who were in the arts whose therapists suggested they try another profession, not because they were meticulously trying to wreck their dreams but because they believed it was the best course of action for them. However, my therapists were supportive of my pursuits and extremely encouraging. That made a great difference for me.

Another great role model for me is Barbara Walters. She is an extremely hard worker, doesn't complain, and does it all herself. And she never lets barriers stop or slow her down. She is at the top of her game, but even with her stature as a journalist, she still faces ageism and sexism. She has had to face many obstacles in the course of her career, but nothing seems to bother her. It's amazing. She's amazing. Through her, you can see what it takes to be a successful woman.

HARRY BELAFONTE

LET THEM HEAR YOU SING

*I learned that the purpose of art is not to show life as it is
but to show life as it should be, and that if art were put into
the service of the human family, it could only enhance it.*

Having come from an extremely dysfunctional family, as a young man I found myself in search of guidance. The guidance offered to me was rather meager. My mother, Millie, was a single parent. Although she was still married to my father, he was absent. In raising us, she did the best she could.

She told us that life was guided by values and wisdom. However, there were areas about growing up where she could not offer very much instruction. The little she did give was very meaningful to me.

So I searched for guidance. I walked through life seeking wisdom and truth, but many of the places I went I found barren and devoid of meaning. These were difficult times for me. So much seemed out of reach.

I volunteered for the navy when I was seventeen, served two years, and at nineteen found myself back on the streets of New York searching for something to become. Quite by accident, I stumbled into the theater.

I first saw *Home Is the Hunter* at Harlem's American Negro Theatre in 1946. It was directed by the artistic director and cofounder of the theater, Abram Hill. It was a profoundly moving experience. Here was a black play, written by a Harlem playwright. It changed my life. I saw purpose, passion, and the impact the play had on the other theatergoers. I knew that I needed to get involved with this theater group.

The American Negro Theatre, located at the 135th Street Library with a capacity of 125 people, was founded in 1940 by Abram Hill and Frederick O'Neal with the goal of eliminating the barriers of black participation in the theater and portraying a more realistic and honest view of black life. In addition to staging productions, the theater also served as a drama school and broadcast a weekly radio program. Community-oriented, the American Negro Theatre was an amazing place to be as a young black man in the 1940s.

The first play in which I performed there was *On Striver's Row,* a satire on social climbing. It was written and directed by Abram Hill and proved a huge success for the theater. The next play in which I acted was Sean O'Casey's *Juno and the Paycock,* an Irish play Hill had reworked to reflect the black American experience. It was brilliantly constructed and very successful. But it was the content of the play that appealed to me. I felt it was an act of social activism to perform it. The original illustrated the plight of the Irish against injustice and the difficulties they faced in their day-to-day lives. Reworked by Hill, it said a great deal about black life in America.

Paul Robeson saw the show in our first week of performance. Afterward he talked with the cast and offered his support and criticism. Meeting the man changed my life. Robeson, the son of a runaway slave and an abolitionist, was a brilliant athlete, scholar, valedictorian at Rutgers University, and law graduate from Columbia University. He took a job in a law firm but quit the legal profession after a white secretary refused to take dictation from him. He turned his intellect and passion to the arts and social activism. He was a humanist, committed to the principles of the Constitution, and a quintessential Renaissance man. He spoke and sang fluently in fourteen languages!

I saw embodied in Paul Robeson everything I wanted to measure my life against. His political and social courage challenged me to better myself in all aspects of my life. As time went on, we became very good friends. It was from Paul that I learned that the purpose of art is not to show life as it is but to show life as it should be, and that if art were put into the service of the human family, it could only enhance it.

He was blacklisted by the House Un-American Activities Committee, which confiscated his passport, citing that he was a Communist. He fought the committee's action and eventually triumphed. His victory was a milestone for many Americans.

I was extremely blessed by his presence in my life. Had it not been for Paul, my life would have been much different. He continually inspired me to do more, to always push myself, and to help as many people as I could in the continual struggle against injustice, not only in America but worldwide. He was a true citizen of the world who cared nothing for political boundaries but always strove to help people everywhere.

Toward the end of his life, I asked him if all his struggles had been worth it. He said to me, "Harry, make no mistake, there is no aspect of what I have done that wasn't worth it. Although we may not have achieved all the goals we set for ourselves and although some victories may have eluded us, the most important aspect was the journey itself and the people I met along the way and the friendships shared."

The one-hundred-year anniversary of his birth was marked in 1998. The celebration that took place at Carnegie Hall was filled with others, like me, whose lives were changed and inspired by this amazing, remarkable, and special man.

TONY BENNETT

THREE DISTINGUISHED MEN
IN MY LIFE

I grew up during the Depression. My father died when I was ten, and my mother raised all three of us while she worked as a seamstress. On Sundays all of our relatives would come for dinner, and after the meal they would form a circle around us kids and we would entertain them. Those Sundays singing with my family inspired me to become a performer, and after more than sixty years I love to sing as much as when I was a child. During the Depression all eyes were on President Roosevelt. He created a sense of community and renewed hope for those who had lost faith in the American Dream. When I was growing up, he represented to many Americans their only hope for the future.

I also witnessed the inspiring example of Dr. Martin Luther King Jr., who, like Franklin D. Roosevelt, knew the importance of words. Another political leader I admire is Mario Cuomo, whom I met many years ago in front of the Hyatt Hotel in Manhattan. I walked up to him and said, "Sir, my name's Tony Bennett and I'm a singer." But before I could finish my introduction he beamed and said, "Boulevard of Broken Dreams," which was my first single. Cuomo, a humanitarian like Roosevelt and King, has the unique ability to bring diverse people together. I think he is able to accomplish this because he has that special gift of understanding government's responsibility to those in need. It is no surprise to me that Mario Cuomo also grew up in the Depression and has likely benefitted from the same Roosevelt policies that I did. His message, again like Roosevelt and Martin Luther King, spoke to a better world and each citizen's responsibility to help build a better America.

There is a common thread through each of these individuals: an appreciation for who we are and who we can become. They helped me understand this and inspire all of us to fight apathy, to fully participate in the democratic process, and to assume a personal stake in the well-being of our world.

These three distinguished men are my role models. They demonstrate that the American Dream is still alive.

Mayor Michael Bloomberg

DINNER TABLE LESSONS

Some people meet their mentors in a classroom. Others, on a play-ing field or in the office. I met mine at the dinner table, every night, growing up in Medford, Massachusetts.

I was lucky to come from a loving, middle-class family, and while I remember teachers and Boy Scout leaders and employers who chal-lenged and inspired me, my greatest mentors—the people who taught me the values that have guided me all through my life—were Charlotte and William Bloomberg, my mother and father.

When I was growing up, dinner was a very important part of the day. My mother cooked, while my sister, Marjorie, and I set the table. We were expected to pitch in, and we did. After my father got home from his job as a bookkeeper at a local dairy, we would sit down for a family meal—and my mother would always use the good china. To her, there was nobody more important than family—so why save the best for someone else?

That was one life lesson learned at the dinner table.

Another was watching my father sit there one evening and write a check to the NAACP.

My father believed in hard work and took great pride in his job. But he felt it was extremely important to give back to others. When I asked him why he wrote the check, he told me, "Because discrimination against anyone is a threat to all of us."

My parents knew about discrimination. They were not able to directly purchase the house that I grew up in because Jews were not welcome buyers. The property was sold first to my parents' lawyer, who then turned around and sold it to them. They never talked about the episode, probably to protect us from feeling hurt and confused and resentful. But also because, I suspect, both of them approached life by looking forward, not backward. And by focusing on the good, rather than dwelling on the bad.

That's what my mother did when my father died, rather suddenly, while I was in college. Though she was devastated (as were we all), she was a pillar of strength, and she went back to work to help support herself and us.

No surprise. This was the woman who had graduated from New York University in 1929, a time when very few women—especially those who were not wealthy—even considered attending college. My mother was always independent and strong-willed—and remains so to this day. On January 2, 2010, she celebrated her 101st birthday.

I owe my best qualities to my parents: a strong will and an independent streak from my mother; and a passion for hard work from my father. But those are only the most outward reflections of my parents that I carry with me every day. Their belief in the importance of family, giving back, treating everyone equally, and looking forward are values that have shaped every major decision I've made in life, and they have given me greater rewards than I ever could have imagined.

ANDREA BOCELLI

MY MENTOR

This essay is adapted from Andrea Bocelli's memoir,
The Music of Silence. *In the book, Bocelli's mentor,*
Amos Martellacci, is named Ettore, and Bocelli is named
Amos in honor of his mentor.

Those who believe in friendship and have faith in their fellow humans usually present themselves to the world with such a positive and open demeanor as to immediately attract an amiable and respectful response from others and immediately quell any doubts. This leads their relationships to develop along the perfect tracks of correct and friendly behavior. Faith is a precious charisma that leads to happiness: so a blind man is happy who has faith in the space that surrounds him, as is the deaf man who has faith in the harmony that accompanies him. A man who has faith in himself and in his fellow man is happy and thanks every day that passes.

This, at least, is what Amos already understood then, albeit in a rather confused fashion. Later he would make sense of the concept that, through his own personal experiences, became almost a philosophy of life for him, a creed, which he would never regret and which he would always hold dear. What is more, as he matured, Amos gradually became convinced that while every man distinguishes himself by his own qualities, all men resemble each other in their defects, which may be more or less pronounced in each individual but are universal.

This thought directed Amos toward tolerance and understanding, to take a long and tortuous road which forced him to restrain his compulsive and passionate nature but which was rich in wonderful surprises.

It was during this period of his life that something very importat happened which constituted a decisive turning point in his spiritual development. The young student who helped him with his reading and his homework every day had taken her degree and then decided to marry a local boy and leave the area. This left Amos with the task of finding a new reader immediately, as the year of the exams for the final diploma was soon coming up. There was no time to waste. On the other hand, it was not easy to find a bright, capable, and willing girl like her who would get to know Amos quickly and understand his difficulties and needs and who could master his particular way of learning. Everyone in the family was concerned and tried to think of who might be able to help, asking around and seeking information.

In the course of a long, sleepless night a solution to this dilemma presented itself to Amos's mother in the name of Ettore. Ettore had retired only a few days earlier from his position as director of the Banca Popolare Agricola of Lajatico. Everyone thought this was too early a retirement for a man of his age and energy, and she immediately saw her idea as being a clever solution albeit an extremely complex one to implement.

Ettore was a unique individual, endowed with exceptional human and intellectual qualities and still healthy and strong. Ettore was really a man outside the norm, in every way, but no one had a word to say against him. Quite the contrary: In fact, everyone respected and admired him for his capabilities and also for his generosity in advising and helping anyone in need.

Ettore taught Amos to question everything, dismantling every certainty, every preconceived notion, every form of youthful fanaticism. He sowed in him the seed of doubt, which at first provokes anguish and bewilderment but later turns into an intoxicating and joyful freedom.

Not only does doubting help one to grow, above all it frees one from the unbearable slavery of needing to be right at all costs. And so gradually Amos began to feel a sense of equanimity and peace which he had never felt before. He also felt stronger and more courageous because that sense of peace provides a unique bastion which gets stronger each time it is attacked and cannot be overcome if not by the conscience that placed it there and thereby has knowledge of all its secrets.

From Ettore, Amos never received praise or signs of esteem, and yet he felt for him an affection that rapidly grew, fed by that extraordinary strength and dedication which his improvised tutor employed for the general good.

One day, during a walk along the river, Ettore said to Amos, "It takes great strength to produce both good and evil, but to do good requires more of it because good is to evil like building is to destroying, and the former is much more demanding than the latter. Good and evil are in the hands of the powerful, but those who do good are stronger even if often they don't get noticed and work in the shadows. Always remember that humanity advances on their shoulders."

Amos would never forget those words.

In Bremen, Ettore attended one of Amos's performances for the first time, and at the end of the concert he came to congratulate him, shaking his hand warmly. Who knows what Amos would have given to know exactly what sensations were felt by that lionheart of a man, sitting in the audience, when he saw him go up onstage next to a famous conductor, to perform for all those expert music lovers who lived for music and were able to make hundreds of discerning comparisons and hard judgments. Who could know if once again Ettore had found time to observe all those concentrated faces and to analyze them with his usual sharp insight, or whether he had abandoned himself to the music, listening with emotion and feeling profoundly moved? Amos would never know.

MAYOR CORY BOOKER

LOVE AND INSPIRATION
LIVE FOREVER

"It is a remarkable gift to tell a child again and again that they are born for a great purpose and that they have a great destiny—it gives them great expectations for their life and a sense of destiny to which they can continuously aspire."

My grandfather was one of my most important mentors. He was larger than life; he was a living inspiration and challenged me through his love to live my best life. This was the most extraordinary gift to all his grandchildren—he instilled in us a belief that we were destined for greatness and born with a profound purpose: He made us believe in the genius of our dreams and that there was nothing we could not accomplish.

Everything my grandfather did was bold, proud, and loud—not one of us could enter a room without him becoming animated with focus and attention, yelling words of encouragement and pronouncements of praise. For me, he would call me "Cory the Great" with such a sense of certainty that I believed it. I was teased by other family members because, as a young toddler, I repeated my grandfather's insistences—"I'm Cory the Great!" Each one of his grandchildren was made to feel special, believing our grandfather saw within us something amazing, believing we had buried within us a destiny that he knew about, celebrated, and repeated over and over. He had us convinced and made us have a belief that was fundamental to success in any endeavor, a belief in ourselves.

My grandfather never hid from us the difficult challenges he endured in his life—the painful stories of poverty, racism, and frustrating failures were always told in a way that conveyed powerful lessons and taught us to rejoice in life and face hardship with perseverance and injustice with a determination to make things right. Importantly, my grandparents didn't just tell us how much they loved us, they showed their love through unyielding, unconditional, indefatigable actions. They looked into our hearts every time we were with them and saw a truth within us that we hadn't discovered fully yet. It has been said that if you see a child as he is, that is all he will ever amount to; but if you see a child as he should be, could be, and will be, that child will forever rise to that vision. My grandfather gave us love to nurture our roots, and like a powerful sun full of brilliance and light, he challenged us to rise to the heavens.

Now this isn't to say that he didn't admonish us, show his disappointment, or have to be strict. There was some powerful discipline dished out by my elders, but in retrospect, my grandfather and family did it just right. They never belittled our spirits and, even when correcting us, would always affirm their vision of who we were. It was never "that was stupid"; it was "you know better than that." It was not "look at you and how horrible you did"; it was "we know you are capable of more." I never heard, "You are bad"—a painful conclusion placed upon a spirit in formation; instead it was, "Cory, this is not acceptable to us, and it shouldn't be acceptable to you."

My grandfather gave us powerful armor to enter the world with and a core of self-respect and love to endure the trials of the world. He gave us a foundation of love that helped us to accept ourselves and thereby accept and love others.

My grandfather is no longer with us physically, but he left a profound message. As I visited my grandfather for the last time and told him that I loved him, he said something to me that I didn't really understand at the time: He responded by saying, "I love you, too. I will always love you and your children and your children's children." I thought pain medication had made him somewhat delusional, as I didn't have children. But months later, on the campaign trail in my first race for mayor, I was called and told that he had died—I sat right where I was and wept at the news. I missed him so (and still miss him to this day), but in my tears and pain something struck me. Maybe I was looking for comfort and was reading too much into it, but I remembered his last words to me and saw meaning. My grandfather didn't live to see me have children or grandchildren of my own, but when he did live, his love was so great and so strong that it will be felt by them one day. He loved so much that generations unborn will feel his love; he loved so much and believed in life so strongly that his service and insistence in the beauty, dignity, and greatness of all God's children will never die and will benefit more people than maybe he even imagined. People may die, but their true love is eternal. My mentor's name may one day be forgotten, but he and his impact will live, generation to generation, forever. I love you, Granddad; I love you, Limuray Jordan.

BILL BRADLEY

GOOD HABITS
LAST A LIFETIME

One person outside my family who played a significant role in my life and who served as my mentor was Ed Macauley, a former basketball player in the National Basketball Association. At a lecture on basketball that I attended when I was fourteen, he said, "If you're not practicing, remember: Someone else somewhere is practicing, and given roughly equal ability, if you two meet, he will win." His words stayed with me and gave me the incentive to work endlessly on my game.

This experience gave me a perspective on the game I loved. My parents could not really provide this because they did not have much informed interest in basketball and therefore could not share my passion for playing.

Ed helped me to establish work habits in every area of my life—habits that last a lifetime, for, as a friend says, Ed's lesson is the origin of my workaholism.

JAMES BRADY

THE IMPORTANCE OF MAKING
A GOOD IMPRESSION

My mother, Dorothy Brady, first involved me in politics and the Boy Scouts. She was the first female elected to the position of precinct committeeman of the state of Illinois.

Her primary responsibilities included voter registration and transporting voters to the polls—she would pick them up at their houses and drive them there. It was an early lesson in organization for me. She had everything accounted for and always emphasized the importance of organization.

My mom got me involved in the Boy Scouts, where I eventually became a Distinguished Eagle Scout. For me, it was an early start in doing good deeds and putting other people before myself, because scouting is about helping people and accomplishing goals through teamwork. My mom was a certified social worker who instilled in me the importance of community service and involvement. She also encouraged me to enter all types of contests. Whether at the local, state, or national level, she would tell me to get an entry form. It didn't matter whether I was good at what the contest called for, it was important just to enter and try one's best to succeed. It was a great educational experience that benefitted me throughout my personal and professional career.

My father was six-foot-two and a yardmaster for the Burlington Railroad (also called the Q by railroad people). He put trains together to be filled at the coal mines in Sesser and Waltonville, Illinois. They would join one hundred hopper cars in the rail yard and take the trains to the mines to be filled with coal; then the coal would go all over the country. The Southern Rail also came through our town on its way to the mines.

If my dad knew the engineer, he would occasionally take me on the train to the mines. We would ride in the big steam-powered locomotives, this being the days before the diesel locomotives. We would travel up to Waltonville, and my dad would tell me all sorts of train trivia and history as he talked with the engineer. He knew all the locomotives: their features, history, and evolution. We would watch the coal being loaded tender by tender until they filled the water tank, and then we'd travel back home.

My father taught me the lesson of hard work. He would get up at 4:30 A.M., fix his own breakfast, and walk to work. He would always rather walk than drive.

I knew when he would get off work, and I would wait for him by the tracks. We would walk home together, and he would tell me all that had happened at the rail yard that day.

My mother somehow saw to it that I was employed by Senate Majority Leader Everett McKinley Dirksen, of Illinois. In my pre-college days, I served as an aide on his staff. My job consisted of serving as a liaison between Mr. Dirksen and the Illinois county fair administrators. At every county fair, each political group was designated a particular night for their representatives to speak. On Republican night, for instance, the Republican candidates and politicians were expected to show up and speak at the fair. The same was granted for the Democrats. If the politicians didn't speak in certain counties, it was their political death sentence. My job was to meet with the county fair representatives and smooth things over if Mr. Dirksen was going to miss a particular fair. It wasn't always a fun job, but I learned a great deal about the importance of communicating with your constituents.

I went to the University of Illinois at Urbana-Champaign, where I became active in government as a student senator. I had learned to set up a campaign from my mother, who taught, of course, that political success all came down to organization. I found that her system worked in student campaigns and, as I later discovered, in state and national campaigns as well.

On an airplane, certain gauges show that you are in the air. For the plane to be moving, the needles on those gauges have to be moving. I've always tried to focus on movement, on getting that gauge to show that you are flying, because if the needle isn't moving, you're not going anywhere.

I still feel my mom pushing me to keep going forward. It's probably a combination of my mother, father, and God. My mom probably has heaven organized by now. I'm sure it was organized before, but not Dorothy D. Brady organized.

Our time on earth can go two ways: It can be like putting your hand in a bucket of water or leaving a solid impression. When you put your hand in the water, it only makes a ripple. There's no impression. I've always tried to make an impression, for which I credit my parents.

HELEN GURLEY BROWN

I STILL LOOK UP TO MY MOTHER

I was born in Green Forest, Arkansas (population three hundred), grew up in Little Rock, and moved to Los Angeles as a teenager. My mother, Cleo Gurley, was the earliest influence in my life, and her encouragement was vital to me both as a child and an adult. Like my father, Ira Gurley, she was a teacher. Unlike my father, she was what you call an early feminist, while he voted against women's suffrage. He asked her not to work after they were married, declaring that no wife of his would work, although they could have used the money and she loved her job.

She quit teaching and fairly soon gave birth to her first baby, my sister Mary, and then me. She poured all the energy she had given to teaching into raising Mary and me.

My parents were intelligent; both had attended college, my father graduating from law school, and I inherited their love of learning. Like my mother, my father encouraged me to be the best at anything I tried. I remember his helping me, paragraph by paragraph, write an essay for a school contest entitled "What Cotton Means to Me." I was nine years old. My father died when I was ten and, quite naturally, my mother became the main influence in my life.

Her guidance was quite different in the ways most mothers of that era influenced their daughters. By frequently warning me through the years not to get married and have children too soon, she emphasized the importance of using my intelligence. With her encouragement, I ran for student government, participated in any contest I could find, and tried out for school plays. I really can't say she was a role model, since she was never able to fulfill her potential in her career, but she was definitely a mentor, someone I looked up to and tried to please.

All this time I was growing up, little girls were supposed to be cute—little princesses, curly-haired, and preferably blonde. Although my mother wanted my sister and me to look nice and spent a mountain of time making our clothes on her trusty Singer sewing machine, she never failed to emphasize the development of the mind, beaming at good report cards and helping with our homework if requested.

In high school a bad case of acne was the blight of my life, but my mother helped me move beyond this scourge. Rather than becoming a recluse, I gathered the courage to be outgoing, involving myself in activities even more and making friends.

Throughout school, a few teachers recognized my writing talent, but no one had the same overwhelming impact on me as my mother. Writing stories and poetry and keeping a diary were interests that she encouraged.

After high school I didn't have too many choices for the future—money was scarce. After graduating (president of the Scholarship Society, class valedictorian—Cleo's influence!), I attended business college for a few months to learn to type and take shorthand. I paid my tuition by working for an announcer at KHJ, a radio station. Salary: six dollars per week. After that, I had jobs at many different corporations working as a secretary.

Not being able to send me to college broke my mother's heart, but she always encouraged me to work hard at whatever I was doing, not just because we needed the money—she never pushed that aspect of my work—but because she wanted me to use my brain. I don't know if she would have wanted me to take it this far, but through the years, I have always enjoyed work more than play. Yes, it's brought money, but more important, recognition and satisfaction.

At age thirty-six I met my husband, David Brown, who turned out to be another important mentor. When I was having a bit of a shaky time in my copywriting job, I asked if he could think of a book I might write, and he suggested that I write about being single. That book became *Sex and the Single Girl*. It was a big bestseller and on the *New York Times* bestseller list for six months.

We never expected such a reaction but were thrilled when it happened. So much mail poured in from young women that David suggested I start a magazine and answer everyone at one time. The two of us put together a format, and he took it all over New York but did not find a publisher. However, he interested the Hearst Corporation in letting us try our format on its once illustrious, but then failing, *Cosmopolitan*.

The corporation gave me a year to make good, but the magazine took off with our first issue. David was never coeditor, but there wouldn't have been any "new Cosmo" if he hadn't helped me sell the idea to a publisher and if he hadn't continued to be involved with its publication for the thirty-two years I was editor in chief. He wrote the cover blurbs for every single issue during my reign.

We all have different types of friends—girl, boy, work, social—and sometimes they overlap. But I would hope everyone has at least one friend who can help him or her in a career. *Mentor* is a rather heavy-sounding word, implying a serious commitment, but a mentor can simply be someone you go to for advice, talk over ideas with, or share your hopes, dreams, and ambitions. All you need is a friend who is interested in you and your career, who knows a lot about the professional world you are in or hope to get into, and will be there to offer guidance and advice.

RICHARD CHAI
GUARDIAN ANGELS

It's hard for me to pinpoint one mentor—having had a series of mentors over the years who were a big influence on my life. From my childhood, my parents were obviously a great influence on me. My father came to the United States from Korea to get a PhD in chemical engineering from Columbia University. His work ethic and dedication to work and our family taught me the importance of working hard and taking pride in what one does.

My mother was a painter and we were always surrounded by the arts. She noticed early on that I was artistic and encouraged this interest. There weren't, however, many art programs in my middle school in Saddle River, New Jersey. I had wanted to be an architect since I was ten. I was inspired by the concept of how two-dimensional lines became three-dimensional forms.

My mother had done some research and suggested I take some night classes at Parsons School of Design in New York City. I was thirteen at the time. We looked through the Parsons catalog of courses, but there were no classes for architecture; the closest thing I could find was graphic design. I thought: It deals with line and composition, so why not? It wasn't until I started the class that I realized it wasn't for me. I didn't understand why it made a difference when something went on the right-hand side of a page versus the left-hand side. I suppose it all felt a bit too technical.

One day there was a sign on the elevator that the graphic design class was moved to another floor. I got into the elevator, dreading going to class. Suddenly, the elevator opened on another floor and I heard super-loud house music and a professor talking in an animated, exaggerated voice. There was a model posing on a platform in the middle of the room as all the students were frantically drawing her. The energy and pulse coming from that classroom were overwhelming. The elevator door soon closed on my face and there I was, reluctantly going to my uninspiring graphic design class.

While in my graphic design class, I kept wondering about the class I had just seen. When we had a break, I ran back to the other classroom and learned that it was fashion illustration and model drawing. I spoke to the professor, Eduard Erlikh, and asked if I could switch into his class. He agreed and the following week I started. Even though I was only thirteen, it was that moment on the elevator that made me realize I wanted to be a fashion designer.

Eduard Erlikh was the first mentor who inspired and encouraged me to become a fashion designer. After I had taken a few classes, my mother spoke to my professor and asked him, "Is this really something my son should pursue?" He replied, "No matter what you think your child is meant to be, I'm telling you he's meant to be a fashion designer." From that point on, everything in my life was about going to Parsons, the school for fashion. I studied and read about fashion because I knew I wanted to be a designer.

As I neared the end of my first year at Parsons, at age eighteen, I started sending résumés to fashion companies to try to get a summer internship. I got a few callbacks, but in the end I got a highly coveted internship at Geoffrey Beene working under Alber Elbaz, the head designer at the time. Geoffrey Beene, or "Mr. Beene" as we were to call him, was one of the greatest American designers of our time and one of the few American couturiers. His aesthetic was architectural, structural, thoughtful, and exquisite. He focused on the integrity of the garment and the craft of making clothes. Sometimes it took four months to finish one dress. It wasn't about mass production at all.

Working for Alber at Geoffrey Beene was one of the most incredible and defining experiences for me as a young fashion student. There was such a graciousness and kindness to him. I recall hanging on to every word from him, because he was so inspiring to me. He treated me like an equal even though I was just an eighteen-year-old intern.

Since that time, Alber has gone on to have an incredible career and is one of the most influential designers in the world. He is the artistic director of Lanvin, and three years ago I made it a point to go see him at a Barney's event honoring him. I said to him, "I'm here to see you and to thank you. I want to thank you for giving me such an amazing opportunity." I don't think he realized how much he influenced me, not only as a designer but as a person. He made the fashion industry so human. I'm a highly sensitive person, and being in this industry at times can be extremely tough. I've always remembered his thoughtfulness, and it's stuck with me to this day and has influenced how I run my own company.

I have been so fortunate in my career to have worked for such amazing designers as Donna Karan and Marc Jacobs and to have become a creative director of TSE before starting my own line. We have many dreams about who we want to be, but it's our mentors who help mold us. What makes these dreams possible is meeting all these influential people along the way. These mentors are truly like guardian angels.

Work hard, have pride in what you do, and be thoughtful and considerate to others. These amazing teachers and mentors have instilled these ideals in me. All of which has contributed a great deal to who I am today—both as a person and as a designer. It's so important to me to extend these same ideals and lessons to those who are around me.

PRESIDENT WILLIAM JEFFERSON CLINTON

KEEP YOUR EYES AND EARS OPEN

After more than sixty years, I'm still being mentored in life and work—by Hillary, Chelsea, friends, coworkers, people I just come across, often in the poorest places on earth.

My fortunate, improbable journey was made possible by the influence and guidance of great mentors—men and women whose actions, encouragement, advice, and example shaped my life.

My grandparents, Edith and Eldridge Cassidy, along with my mother, were my constants. Their unconditional love and confidence gave me confidence to dream big dreams, work hard to achieve them. They also kept me grounded and never let me forget that I was no better than anyone else and that I should treat all people with respect and try to learn something from them. My grandfather ran a grocery store when I was very young. I vividly recall the way he treated all of his customers, black and white, with kindness and respect. Despite the fact that the South was segregated, I was raised to see all people as equals. I learned this not because of what my parents said but because of what they did. My grandmother organized my preschool learning in reading and arithmetic. My grandfather sparked my compassion and interest in other people's lives. He made me want to help other people live their dreams, too.

When I was a student at Georgetown's School of Foreign Service, I found a way to think about how to do that. In his history of civilization class, Professor Carroll Quigley said America became the greatest nation in history because our people had always believed in the two pillars of Western civilization: that tomorrow can be better than today and that every one of us has a personal moral obligation to make it so. I've lived my entire life with these words in mind.

While I was at the White House, actually trying to build a better future for America and the world in a highly partisan atmosphere, I was mentored by Nelson Mandela, who taught me that one can serve well only when the mind and heart are focused on the work at hand and on the real lives that will be affected. He said persistent attacks and unfair treatment are the price of fighting for change, but if you devote your mind and heart to obsessing about them, you give up your freedom to do good and to be happy. He came out of twenty-seven years in prison a stronger, greater man than he was when he went in. He said his transformation began when he realized his tormentors could take everything from him "except my mind and my heart. Those things I would have to give them. I decided not to give them away. And neither should you." It may be the best advice I ever got.

After more than sixty years, I'm still being mentored in life and work—by Hillary, Chelsea, friends, coworkers, people I just come across, often in the poorest places on earth. My grandparents were right: If you keep your eyes and ears open and treat people with respect, it's amazing what you can learn and how you can keep growing.

KENNETH COLE

MAYBE SOMEDAY I CAN FILL MY FATHER'S SHOES

My father, Charles Cole, would wake me up at 5:00 many Saturday mornings, starting when I was ten. He would invite me into his world, a world that he didn't share with many people. At 5:30 we would have breakfast and talk about what was happening in my world. Then we would go to his shoe factory in lower Manhattan, and I would sit with him in his office and watch him as he worked.

He served in the marines in World War II and was stationed in the South Pacific. He was a tough guy, very strong willed, and a hands-on businessman. He would be in the factory opening cartons and in the office opening mail. He knew each step of the manufacturing process and what was written on every piece of paper.

He was very much of the "do as I do" mentality, not only to me but to all the people who worked there. He inspired everyone around him and took a personal interest in the lives of all the people he worked with. His passion for business was not that much different than his approach to everything in his life.

In the early 1970s, I went to Emory University in Atlanta for my undergraduate degree with the intention of attending law school. As I was about to embark on my legal education, my father's right-hand man left the factory to start a competitive business.

To help my father, I put off law school to learn the business as quickly as I could. I knew that in order to succeed I would need the support and respect of everyone in the company, including my father. But not having enough experience and knowledge, I realized I couldn't impress them with the quality of my work. So I set out to show them what I could with the quantity of my work. If the first worker arrived at 6:30 A.M., I would arrive at 6:15.

I found myself fascinated with the production process from beginning to end. I seemed to always gravitate to the sample room, where the product was designed and manufactured, understanding that this was the nucleus of the business. Then I would find the time to help open the mail or sweep the floor.

I became fascinated with the concept of transforming an idea into a new style of shoe. With my father's encouragement, I took it upon myself to create my own collection of footwear, different from anything the factory had ever made. Open to creative alternatives and anxious to further encourage me, my dad then suggested I visit the principal industry publication, *Footwear News,* and on the way back bring the samples to some important buyers. *Footwear News* proceeded to write a story in the next edition about a new up-and-coming designer, and each customer who saw the shoes bought some. I was off and running.

I loved that the rewards for those efforts were so quick in coming and that there were no specific rules. I realized that if I had chosen to study the law, I would always be judged by my legal knowledge in contrast to what I was doing, where no rules existed. I knew that the further I went beyond what had been done before, the more likely I would succeed.

Over the next five years, my father and I built a successful business together. I then realized that I needed to take on the ultimate challenge of starting my own business. I did it confidently with his encouragement and never looked back. I was lucky that so early in my career I had such a great role model who gave me the tools to be successful, the practical experience on how to use them, and the courage to trust my instincts.

I made great strides in a very competitive field, but I reached a point when it all started to become a little empty. I needed to find a way to make things more relevant. I knew that if I were going to continue to give so much of myself I would have to find a way to make it part of something bigger. So early on in the company's development, I decided to make the awareness of meaningful social issues an important part of the company's culture, so that "what one stands for is more important than what they stand in," and that "to be aware is more important than what you wear." These principles would eventually become part of the company's philosophy.

My father, my mentor, by his example, was a testament of the value of hard work and the concern for one's fellow human beings. He did everything with all of his heart as well as his "sole."

CINDY CRAWFORD
THANKS FOR THE MENTORING

I have been blessed throughout my life by encountering people who have enabled me to grow and develop as an individual.

First and foremost, my mother has always given me her unconditional love and support. She has always had great faith in me, and with her inherent strength of character, she challenged me to fulfill my dreams. Even during her divorce from my father she had a positive outlook on life. She explained to me that when you try your best there is no failure: "You can always come home again. Failure is when you do not try at all."

My father also had a great deal of influence on me. He inspired me to be ambitious and to develop a love of learning. He also challenged me and consistently emphasized that girls could accomplish as much as, or more than, boys.

I was fortunate to have great teachers every year in school. In fourth grade I had a student teacher determined to confer nicknames on her students. I was dubbed "Future Miss America." She helped me to understand that beyond the confines of my hometown there was a whole world of possibilities to explore.

Mr. Halvorson, my high school calculus teacher, was an exceptional person. I appreciated the fact that he was both an authority figure and a friend. He emphasized that the world is a bigger place than our familiar neighborhood. He filled his students with excitement and anticipation for the future. Mr. Halvorson also taught me a strong lesson—that learning can be fun.

Looking back on my career, I realize that modeling has changed throughout the years and that I have been a real part of that change. In Chicago, a photographer, Victor Skrebneski, stands out among the myriad people that have affected this important facet of my life. When I was eighteen, he recognized my potential and gave me counseling that would last a lifetime. First, he told me to regard modeling as a profession and a job, not a lifestyle. Second, he told me that my job as a model was to make the clothes of the client look as good as possible. When Victor taught me that modeling was a job and "not about me," I was realistic about the career path I was undertaking.

When I was twenty, I decided to move to New York City to further my career. I was already equipped with valuable tools and lessons that would serve me well. My job skills included discipline, being on time, and doing the best work I could. Payment was commensurate to the quality of performance.

I have been fortunate to know extraordinary individuals who have consistently been strong influences on my life. They have challenged me and empowered me to develop my talents and become successful. I cannot remember a year when I did not have their sage counsel and encouragement when needed. All of these wonderful people enabled me to be who I am today.

WALTER CRONKITE

EVERYONE YOU WRITE ABOUT
IS A HUMAN BEING

I went to San Jacinto High School in Houston, Texas, in the 1930s and was fortunate to come in contact with a man who would inspire me to become a career print and broadcast journalist. Fred Birney was a pioneer in school journalism. Very few high schools at that time even taught journalism, and many schools didn't have their own student newspaper.

Fred talked the Houston Board of Education into allowing him to teach a journalism class once a week at three local high schools, one of which was San Jacinto. He was a newspaperman of the old school and taught us a great deal about reporting and writing. He also became a sponsor of the San Jacinto High School newspaper, the *Campus Cub*. Under his tutelage, we published it monthly, whereas it had previously been published in a casual manner, just three or four times a year. During my junior year, I was the sports editor of the *Campus Cub* and its chief editor in my senior year.

Fred was a hands-on technical teacher, explaining the complexities of layout and copy. He also stressed the importance of the tight lead— the diminished inverted pyramid of an article's development and the necessity of taking an honest approach toward the subject matter.

At the time, I was an avid reader of *American Boy* magazine, which was composed of a series of short stories to inspire boys to follow certain careers. I remember reading an article about mining engineers. I wish I had read an article about petroleum engineering in Texas in the 1930s instead of becoming interested in mineral mining. So here I was about to graduate, and I was torn between becoming a mining engineer and a journalist. Things could have been a lot different for me without Fred.

He was well connected with the three newspapers in Houston. During the summer of my junior year, he secured his interested students jobs as copy boys and girls with the *Houston Post*. Then, after I graduated in 1933, I became the campus correspondent for the *Houston Post* at the University of Texas at Austin and worked at the college paper, the *Daily Texan*, working my way up to become its editor. My sophomore year I got a weekend job working as an exalted copy boy for the *International News Service* at the state capitol, but I was also asked to cover committee meetings of the state legislature.

That same year I was hired as a full-time cub reporter with the Scripps Howard Bureau, where I was taken under the wing of another newsman, Vann Kennedy. He gave me a great deal of advice and tutelage and many chances to cover stories at the capitol.

Texas politics was an interesting arena for a budding journalist because the state legislative committee meetings addressed a number of special interest areas: farming, timber, cotton, mining, and many others. All these groups lobbied the various politicians to advance their own legislative self-interests.

At this time the country was in a time of immense transition. Technology was advancing at a rapid rate, and the money generated by these special interest groups, especially in Texas, was growing rapidly. It was an exciting time to be covering politics at any level.

At the end of my sophomore year, I was offered a job as a full-time reporter at the *Houston Press*. Roy Roussel was the city editor, and his brother Peter was the culture editor. They helped me a great deal, and I learned a lot from them. I was with the *Press* for a year and a half and never returned to college.

I was visiting my grandparents in Kansas City in 1936 when I saw an ad in the *Kansas City Star* for a radio station broadcasting football games in Oklahoma. Radio was new at the time, and it was an exciting opportunity; it was in its primitive stages then—we got the news straight off the wire service. So I applied for the job and was hired to cover University of Oklahoma football games and news for WKY in Oklahoma City. However, the job lacked the excitement of my previous reporting experience.

I covered football until the threat of war became more of a reality. It was then that I realized my need to get back into news reporting. I was hired by the United Press, where I stayed for eleven years and served as a war correspondent during World War II. In 1950 I was hired by CBS and became further involved in radio and television.

Fred Birney wouldn't admire the type of journalism going on today. He was always big on journalistic integrity. "You've got to remember that everyone you write about is a human being," he would tell us, "not just a headline."

We exchanged several letters until his death, shortly after my high school graduation. He taught me so much in those high school classes, and by securing me those early jobs, he cemented my desire to be a reporter for the rest of my life. He was my major inspiration. I always credit Fred Birney for my career.

Governor
Andrew Cuomo

Sons and Daughters
of Giants

Our country was built by immigrants like my grandparents, Andrea and Immaculata Cuomo and Charles and Mary Raffa. They came to this country because of the freedom of opportunity and the promise to provide a better life for their families. They helped me to understand that everyone deserves an opportunity to try their best for success. My grandparents were disciplined, self-sacrificing people who loved and wanted the best for their family. Though my grandfathers, Charles and Andrea, were born in the United States, they were raised in Italy, and returned to this country as adults. They believed that education was a gift that would give us the greatest strength: self-respect. And with self-respect we would become better citizens, better workers, better partners, better parents, and better human beings. They were especially proud to see their grandchildren furthering their learning. My grandparents were not highly educated, but they taught me and enriched my life by sharing many of life's lessons through anecdote and personal example.

As a youth, I recall the wonderful vacations spent at the Raffa summer home at Lake Hopatcong, New Jersey, and the barbecues at the Cuomo home in Holliswood, Queens. Those were always happy events with swimming and boating and lots of food. Their hospitality and warmth made us feel that their homes were ours, too, and that our friends were always welcome.

Holiday celebrations always took place at our house, and my parents maintained the traditions of our grandparents. And of course, my grandparents always participated in these festivities.

One experience I will never forget was when my beloved dog, Sport, was fatally injured by a speeding car. In addition to the loving care and understanding of my parents and siblings, it was Grandfather Andrea who made it easier for me to cope with my sorrow, by choosing a special burial site for Sport in his backyard.

During my father's gubernatorial campaign, all the grandparents visited many senior citizen centers to speak on behalf of my father. Though they were wary of politics, they knew my father would be a good governor and would help people in need. Even in politics, family support made a big difference.

A few years ago, I traveled to Italy, and though I had visited Italy as a child, it was on that trip I recalled vividly and, moreover, *understood* the wonderful stories of my grandparents' Italy, the warmth of the Italian people, and the beauty of Italian culture and tradition.

Our wonderful grandparents left all of us—my sisters Margaret, Maria, and Madeline, my brother Christopher, and me—with a legacy to be true to yourself and your ideals, and if you want to realize your potential and your dreams, a good education is the most important thing. I hope to leave these legacies to my own children. To my grandparents I say: You were the watchtower to my sisters, brother, and me. You were an extension of my parents, and we respect and love you for everything you did for our family. You helped us become the adults we are today. *Mille grazie!*

CHRISTOPHER CUOMO

EVERYONE HAS SOMETHING TO TEACH YOU

I am unusually blessed. I have never had to look very far for mentors; they have always been around me. After all, the word *mentor* means more than just "teacher"; a mentor is someone who guides your development as a person in various ways. From family and friends to the people I meet in the course of covering stories—people who teach me about love and loss and overcoming obstacles—I am always growing.

My mother and father are a constant and consistent example of love in action and commitment to others. Simple instructions like Pop telling me to "Always ask 'Why?'" or my mother cautioning that "How you treat people says the most about you" have traveled with me for forty years. Watching them and learning from the decisions they have made about what matters in life have proven invaluable.

As the youngest, I have grown up watching and learning from my brother and three sisters, as well. They have all built lives and relationships that inspire respect and motivate me to live my own life in a way that emphasizes service to others.

Looking at my life currently, it seems I have surrounded myself with people who are mentors. My wife, Cristina, is a constant reminder of who I would like to be as a parent and spouse. At work, I am part of a team of journalists who are dedicated to the true pursuit of journalism as a way of revealing the lives of others. I have been fortunate enough to work around legendary names like Donaldson, Jennings, Sawyer, and Walters, each of whom has added to my reporting persona.

In fact, all the men and women I call friends live their lives in ways that reflect different values I try to emulate. Some of my friends are incredibly successful in business or are top-notch attorneys while others are leaders in charitable endeavors and many are family-first types who make great sacrifices for their children.

Maybe that is one of the lessons I have learned best: to choose the people in your life wisely. And also to remember that everyone has something to teach you.

Right now, the people I am learning the most from are probably the youngest people in my life: my kids. My daughter, Isabella, has a zest for life that makes me remember to enjoy all I have been given (it's so easy for a reporter to be cynical); my son, Mario, is so caring that he reminds me daily that compassion is the greatest virtue; and little Carolina has a sunny disposition that makes me smile no matter what is going on in my life. And when you think about it, what lessons are more important than those?

GOVERNOR MARIO CUOMO

THE BEST RATIONALE FOR LIVING

The most valuable lesson my role models taught me is that the game is lost only when we stop trying for the greatest excellence of which we are capable.

Because I was born in the middle of the Depression and my parents and older brother and sister were constantly occupied by our family grocery store and their jobs, I had an unusually spare relationship with the members of my family. All of them were bright, hard-working, loving, and generous people, and while we did not have all the time together we would have liked, their influence on me was all good and useful. Outside of my family there were few, if any, individuals who made lasting impressions on me. But there was the world of books.

Over the years, three different heroic figures had the greatest influence on me—Thomas More, Abraham Lincoln, and of course Jesus. In the case of More, I was impressed because he combined the law and public service and religious belief so well. And in the end, he put conscience over consequence to himself.

Lincoln's language fascinated me.

And Jesus offered me—and many millions of others—the best rationale for living.

Actually, these "mentors" intimidated me a bit because they were all so far beyond what I could ever be. But they set examples to admire and strive for. I wound up a lawyer in public life who is still struggling to learn to use language well, to put conscience over consequences, and to understand the world's basic rationale. All of this I have done very imperfectly but better than I would have without my three role models.

The most valuable lesson my role models taught me is that the game is lost only when we stop trying for the greatest excellence of which we are capable. I'm still in the game.

OSSIE DAVIS
FINGERPRINTS

I grew up in Waycross, Georgia, and went to Center High School, where Mr. Lucius Jackson taught chemistry and physics and coached several of the sports teams. In 1934, my parents moved to Valdosta, Georgia, but some of my teachers wanted me to finish my senior year at Center and graduate with my friends. They found a place for me to stay and allowed me to remain with my classmates that year.

Jack, as we called Lucius Jackson, was fond of me. I was a good student and smart enough to finish his chemistry courses a year early. Jack wanted me to go out for the football team, but I felt that I wasn't big enough to play, and temperamentally, I really wasn't a contact person—I didn't want to grab people or be grabbed by them. So he made me water boy, and I went with the team everywhere.

I was also his laboratory assistant and helped teach the laboratory classes in chemistry. One day, an inquisitive and inventive friend of mine and I went to the lab to conduct our own experiment. We added the proper proportions of water, meal, and sugar until we had concocted a rather fine homebrew. Awaiting the time for fermentation to run its course, we ultimately took the proper scientific approach to such an experiment: We drank it. However, the principal at Center took exception to our scientific enthusiasm and wanted to kick us both out of school. Jack intervened on our behalf, saying he would be responsible for us the rest of the year.

Jack first put the idea of college in my mind and prepared the proper mind-set for me to go to school. No one else in my family had gone to college—I would be the first.

I came to Harlem in April 1939 and found my way to the Rose McClendon Players, a local black acting company, where I first met Dick Campbell. He helped me get a job, a place to stay, and even lent me money. It was Dick Campbell who trained me, taking his raw country material and teaching "it" how to walk, talk, sit, stand—everything. More important, he taught me that theater and art were instrumental in the struggle of black people. We performed for the Urban League and at pageants for the NAACP. Theater and performance had a socially responsible aspect to them.

After World War II, Dick became my agent and helped me land my first Broadway role by setting up an audition. After I got the part, he helped negotiate my contract. He surrounded me with other actors who would keep an eye out for me and show me the tricks of the trade.

Both Lucius Jackson and Dick Campbell have indelibly left their fingerprints on me. Although they are dead now, I remained as close as possible to them until their last days. I was a surrogate son for both; neither had any children of their own and looked with a degree of paternal pride on everything that I did. They made a great difference in my life.

DR. DJIBRIL DIALLO

NO OBJECTIVE IS BEYOND REACH

The late James Grant, executive director of UNICEF from 1980 to 1995, is the role model and mentor who continues to inspire me. He was a tireless and effective advocate for children, determined to put child survival, protection, and development on the global agenda.

I worked closely with him as his special assistant for ten years, traveling the world and working at every level, from the offices of presidents to the poorest communities. His efforts were unrelenting, and he could convince people that they have the power to make the world a better place for children.

He helped change the global agenda of development, widening the focus on major infrastructure projects and private investment to include human development, beginning with children. He showed that basic health care, nutrition, education, and empowerment of women and girls are the foundation for progress.

A dramatic illustration of his vision came when he was invited to address heads of state at the Organization of African Unity, predecessor to the African Union, in 1988. Before speaking, he introduced a girl, age twelve, from Ethiopia named Selamawit Gebre-Eyesus, who had lived on the streets with her brother in abject poverty.

She said: "A few years ago, someone asked me what I wanted to be when I grow up. I answered, 'I want to be alive.' Now I wish the same for all children in Africa. So please, help them survive." She personified the need for the revolution for children that James Grant pioneered.

He showed extraordinary commitment and a readiness to think creatively outside the box. For example, the idea of bringing presidents and prime ministers together for a summit devoted to children was unthinkable, even laughable. But Mr. Grant skillfully lobbied key leaders in Africa and other continents, and in 1990 nearly one hundred sixty heads of state and government and high-level officials came together at the United Nations for the World Summit for Children.

They committed to achieve key goals to save the lives of millions of mothers and children through immunization and health care and to ensure that every child is able to go to school. This led to a series of global summits during the 1990s, culminating in the Millennium Summit in 2000, where world leaders agreed on the Millennium Development Goals for 2015. These benchmarks continue to guide our global development efforts.

Without the influence of James Grant, I would most likely still be working in the area of international development. My mother instilled in me the importance of service to society and of education. This was reinforced by Léopold Sédar Senghor, the first president of Senegal when the country became independent in 1960, who emphasized that children should be educated to become global citizens.

But Mr. Grant's example still inspires me. Many of my former colleagues at UNICEF continue to work with the United Nations, and we remind each other that we went to the "Jim Grant school"—meaning that no objective is beyond reach if you keep pushing.

In fact, Michel Sidibé, who was appointed last year as the executive director of UNAIDS (the Joint United Nations Programme on HIV/AIDS), also worked with Mr. Grant. I greatly appreciate the opportunity to work now with Mr. Sidibé.

Globally, new HIV infections have been reduced by seventeen

percent from 2001 to 2009. Yet globally only forty-two percent of those needing treatment receive it, and for every two people starting treatment, five more become newly infected with HIV. More than twenty-two million people are currently living with HIV in sub-Saharan Africa, and every day nearly twelve hundred babies are born HIV-positive.

We need to work harder to reach the goal of universal access to AIDS prevention, treatment, care, and support, and a key target is ending mother-to-child transmission of HIV. We have the means to end such infections by 2015. I know that James Grant would not rest until we have done so—nor can we.

FRAN DRESCHER
DON'T MIX IMAGINATION
WITH FEAR

People come into our lives for a reason. I am blessed my dear friend and manager, Elaine Rich, came into mine so early on. She is the very definition of loyalty, friendship, character, enthusiasm, class, style, and most important love.

Always a wise ol' owl, Elaine has shared with me over the years many amazing anecdotes that have gotten me through some tough and difficult times, from my career all the way to my love life. She always believed in me as an actress and taught me about entertaining and fine art. When I had no money, she assured me I was her blue chip stock, and she paid for my head shots herself!

When I was in my late twenties, I was raped and wasn't able to get in touch with my pain. But Elaine helped me through the horror I faced and the pain I endured. I wanted to leave Los Angeles, and she advised me to wait six months to see if I felt the same way then. Of course I didn't. That devastation made me a stronger person because I had her strength to lean on and her advice to heed.

She has stood up for me on numerous occasions and has been my voice of vigor and vitality that I lacked at times. At one point in my life, I felt betrayed by an industry executive, and I'll never forget when she sided with me in the matter. She told that certain individual, "I don't mind if you stick an umbrella up my ass, but when you open it, you've gone too far!"

When I was told I had cancer, I was terrified, but Elaine gave me advice that will always stick with me. She said, "Fran, don't mix imagination with fear. It's a deadly cocktail." Her words were at once soothing and blunt; tough love with much more love than anything else.

We have traveled the world together—Mexico, Paris, Israel—and along the way we've cherished many memories full of laughter and happiness. For thirty-two wonderful years, I have had her in my life and we have gone through everything together; we've been fat and thin, young and old, happy and sad, rich and poor.

Elaine is an extraordinary woman who has always gone to great lengths to show me what life is all about. She is my mentor, my confidant, and my best friend. Because of her, I know how to live life more completely.

MARIAN WRIGHT EDELMAN

THE YOUNGER GENERATION IS YEARNING TO MAKE A DIFFERENCE

I grew up in Bennettsville, South Carolina, the daughter of a Baptist preacher. My parents had the most important influence on me while I was growing up and are responsible for the values I received as a child. I also fell under the influence of the community elders, who saw themselves as an essential part in the raising of the town's children. It was a role that was expected of them.

I went to Spelman College in Atlanta. It was a staid women's college that developed safe, young women who married Morehouse men, helped raise a family, and never kicked up dust.

My history professor there, Howard Zinn, taught me the value of questioning the status quo and illustrated the power inherent in an individual. Professor Zinn got us involved in the political climate of the times. This was the South of the late 1950s, where the first attempts at social and political change in the struggle for civil rights originated.

Professor Zinn would take us outside the sheltered stone wall of the Spelman gates to the realities of interracial dialogues and protests. The activism we initially took part in preceded the regional and national movements that are usually referred to as the civil rights era.

One of our first actions was to protest the policy of public library segregation. Protesters (predominately college students) walked into the Carnegie Library in Atlanta, asking librarians for such works as John Stuart Mill's *On Liberty* or John Locke's *An Essay Concerning Human Understanding*. Some asked for the U.S. Constitution and others for the Declaration of Independence. Using such tactics, the Atlanta Library Board changed its segregationist policy. It was actions such as these that led to further protests, further questioning, and striving for basic American freedoms. It was the beginning of a movement for many of us.

Professor Zinn was instrumental in helping me get a fellowship for a junior year abroad. He had a lot of faith in me as a young girl and felt that traveling on my own would benefit me more than going with the South or Sweetbriar groups.

I left the United States in 1958 and traveled through Europe for fifteen months. My year abroad gave me the confidence to take risks and follow my own path. It made me more of an individual; it gave me a sense of myself. It also exposed me to the possibilities of the world. There was so much out there, so much to see and experience. My year abroad was a very special time; it was a time of awakening.

I returned to Atlanta to find a more socially and racially tense city. Opinions had grown stronger on both sides, and the consequences of those opinions were taking shape in the worst of ways. Professor Zinn continued to involve students in civil rights issues and led them to more protests and rallies.

It was also at this time that I decided to go to law school. It was something I had never thought of before, but somewhere in the course of my travels it became a reality for me. I graduated from Spelman in 1960 and went to Yale Law School. After receiving my degree I returned to Mississippi to continue my activism with the Student Nonviolent Coordinating Committee, which organized most of the voter registrations and protests for blacks in the Deep

South, many resulting in violent confrontations with small-town law officers and locals.

Professor Zinn responded to a yearning in the younger generation to make a difference, and like all good teachers, he brought out the best in people. He was concerned with justice, and everyone around him caught his concern. He was a very special man whose political activities eventually got him fired from Spelman. He went on to Boston University and became an outspoken critic of the Vietnam War.

Well into his eighties, Professor Zinn remained an optimist. He was a prolific writer of numerous books, including the controversial *A People's History of the United States* and *You Can't Be Neutral on a Moving Train*. I am grateful to him for fostering in me the belief that I could make a difference; it is something I have carried with me ever since.

As I watched Andrew Young being sworn in as the mayor of Atlanta in 1981, I felt such a sense of accomplishment. Before the ceremony, I ate lunch in a cafeteria where I had protested and been arrested years before. I had come full circle.

NORA EPHRON
THE TRUTH OF THE STORY

I had a couple of great, great teachers. The teacher who changed my life was my journalism teacher, whose name was Charles Simms. I always tell this story because I love it. I had already decided that I was going to be a journalist. I didn't know why exactly, except that I had seen a lot of Superman comics with Lois Lane as a reporter. But Mr. Simms really inspired my passion for journalism. He got up on the first day of class, went to the blackboard, and wrote "Who, what, where, why, when, and how," which are the six things that have to be in the lead of any newspaper story. Then he did what most journalism teachers do—he dictated a set of facts to us, and then we were all meant to write the lead that was supposed to have "who, what, where, why, when, and how" in it.

The facts he dictated went something like this: "Kenneth L. Peters, the principal of Beverly Hills High School, announced today that the faculty of the high school will travel to Sacramento on Thursday for a colloquium in new teaching methods. Speaking there will be anthropologist Margaret Mead and Robert Maynard Hutchins, the president of the University of Chicago." We all sat at our typewriters and wrote a lead, most of us inverting the set of facts so that they read something like this, "Anthropologist Margaret Mead and University of Chicago President Robert Maynard Hutchins will address the faculty Thursday in Sacramento at a colloquium on new teaching methods, the principal of the high school, Kenneth L. Peters, announced today."

We were very proud of ourselves, and we gave the leads to Mr. Simms. He looked at what we had written and tore them into tiny bits and tossed them into the wastebasket. And he said, "The lead to this story is: There will be no school Thursday!" It was this great epiphany moment for me about the essence of journalism. I thought, "Oh my God, it is about the point! It is about figuring out what the point is." And I just fell in love with journalism at that moment. I fell in love with the idea that underneath, if you sifted through enough facts, you could get to the point, and you had to get to the point. You could not miss the point. That would be bad. So he really kind of gave that little shift of mind a major push.

A few months later, I entered a city-wide contest to write an essay in fifty words or less on why I wanted to be a journalist. I won first prize, two tickets to the world premiere of a Doris Day movie. Because of Mr. Simms, I fell in love with journalism—with solving the puzzle, figuring out what it was, what was the story, what was the truth of the story.

GLORIA ESTEFAN

DISCOVER WHAT MAKES YOU HAPPY

There is only one person in my life whom I consider a mentor—my grandmother on my mother's side, Consuelo Garcia. Besides her obvious role as a grandparent, she represented to me a vivid example of a woman ahead of her-time. She was a strong, caring, spiritual humanitarian who filled my life with possibilities and through her example gave me the belief that there was nothing I could not do or achieve in life. Although she was born in 1905 in Cuba, she felt no limitations and even aspired to be a lawyer, an unheard-of profession for a Latin woman. And though she had to leave school to help her large family at the age of ten, she taught herself to read and write and became an amazingly astute businesswoman and extremely independent.

She cared for me from birth and nurtured the thought that music was a gift I had received. And although I was reluctant to follow that path, I somehow found myself involved with music, because our gifts are meant to be shared for the good and pleasure of others. We remained extremely close throughout my life, and even after her death I have often found comfort in her memory and the wisdom she shared with me.

It is difficult to pick one specific meaningful experience that we shared, because there were many unusual and uncanny experiences that became commonplace as our lives intertwined more and more. We shared a unique psychic connection, and it became impossible for me to go through difficult situations without my grandmother somehow "knowing." She was very aware of and quite comfortable with this unusual gift and became instrumental in my discovery of my own intuitiveness as well. It is something I have drawn upon in many instances in life.

My grandmother always pointed out my strengths and filled me with hope for the future. She constantly nourished my inquisitiveness and shared many quests for seeking answers to my questions. She wasn't afraid to let me see her vulnerability and made that intimacy an asset to be celebrated. Primarily through her example I learned that we, as women, have limitless potential. I finally said yes to music because of her.

Singing "came with me" into this life, but I was not pursuing it as a career. I studied psychology, communications, and languages, but she repeatedly told me that I would be happiest doing something I loved. Often she would bring people in the music business to listen to me and somehow with gentle prodding try to sway me. But she knew that it would have to be me that chose a musical career. I'm happy to have followed her advice, because she was right. I finally chose the best career for myself.

The turning point in my life came when I auditioned for my band, Miami Sound Machine. I took my mother, sister, and grandmother to the audition. I initially joined the band as a hobby, but my grandmother told me after I had been accepted that I had probably taken the most important step of my life.

The most valuable lessons I learned from my grandmother were to discover what makes you happy and *do* it with as much energy and joy as you can muster. And that success takes perseverance, determination, and an unwavering belief in what you have chosen to do.

I feel fortunate to have found such an amazing mentor. I don't believe that people like my grandmother are commonplace, or even a given within my family. She had a profound influence on who I am and continues to be my inspiration.

SARAH FERGUSON
SURVIVING LIFE'S UNCERTAINTIES

I liken my mother to a winding river that encountered storms and hardship around every turn, yet flowed on with amazing strength and grace.

Without question my mother, Susan Barrantes, was my mentor. When she died tragically in a car crash, it was as if a light had gone out of my life. She was a unique person, and I lost a great friend as well as a fantastic mother.

People are sometimes curious about my relationship with my mother. We lived continents apart since I was barely a teen, yet the truth is that Mum and I always had an uncommonly deep and unbreakable bond. Our love, trust, and mutual respect transcended distance and time because it was so pure, and we remained intimate as a mother and daughter could ever be, right up to the time of her death.

Even as a young girl, I recall my mother's simple, elegant beauty. She had a subtle yet dazzling presence, with an effortless style and an easy cleverness that drew people to her. But for me it was her gentle warmth and boundless energy that I adored most. Mum had a special way of making all things seem possible, and her positive outlook showed me a world that was brimming with color, excitement, and wonder. I suppose that's why I am always looking at the bigger picture in my own life, ever curious and prodding at boundaries to get at what's on the other side.

There was a private side to my mother that also had a tremendous influence on me. Mum was wise, incredibly strong, and full of kindness and compassion. I'll always be amazed by the way that this beautiful Englishwoman followed her heart to a rural ranch in Argentina, where she knew little of the customs and did not speak the language. She was a stranger in a harsh and physically demanding land, but through her openness and caring ways, she was soon embraced by the entire community, and in many ways it was like an extended family to her.

I liken my mother to a winding river that encountered storms and hardship around every turn, yet flowed on with amazing strength and grace. By her example I learned to seize and savor the joys in my life, but it was also her absolute courage and dignity during her most difficult times that taught me the most about facing and surviving life's uncertainties.

GERALDINE FERRARO

MY MOTHER'S BLUEPRINT FOR LIFE

My mother, Antonetta, taught me how to live life. She had experienced many setbacks in her own life yet never let them get the best of her. She lost one child when he was six days old. Another son was killed in an automobile accident when he was three. My father died when my mother was thirty-nine, and some difficult financial times followed as she worked to raise my brother and me. But she never complained, and whenever I suffered a setback she would say, "Deal with the situation, learn from your mistakes, and move on." She was a strong woman who lived a tough life, but she remained an optimist throughout. It was probably that optimism and her devotion to her children that kept her going.

My mother also believed quite strongly that I could become whatever I wanted to be. This was rather unusual for the time and for her culture. Most Italian Americans did not feel that women had options in life. The prevailing notion of the time was that a woman's place was in the home, raising a family. My mother considered that a laudable life choice but only one of many. She saw no reason that a woman's potential should be limited simply because she was born female. She was obviously ahead of her time.

My mother's unwavering belief in me and my ability was the

main reason I was able to succeed. I saw possibilities in everything. Fueled by her encouragement, I launched myself into my studies and found joy in academics. Perhaps because she had to go to work to support younger brothers and sisters when she was thirteen, my mother directed her energies to making certain both my brother and I would have the education that she had been denied. Her work as a crochet beader, hunched over a wooden frame for hours on end, gave me the tools to win scholarships. Her encouragement got me through law school at night. My mother remained the main influence in my life until her death, but when I entered Congress I also acquired a political mentor.

In 1978, I won a seat in the House of Representatives. It was then that I met "Tip" O'Neill. He was not only the Speaker, he was a father figure, a great teacher, and a superb politician. Having lost my own father at a young age, it meant a great deal to me that he would spend time with me. In 1984, Tip was the first person to suggest my name as the Democratic nominee for vice president.

My mother died in 1990, but she left a blueprint for life that I continue to follow. She stressed that I have been blessed by good things in life and that I have an obligation to pay back. She also cautioned that I should never forget where I came from. I've always attempted to do just that. For her.

LAURENCE FISHBURNE

REMAIN OPENHEARTED AND OPEN-MINDED

This was a turning point of my life, for I was able to
understand their passion and realize that I, too,
could pursue an artistic life.

I have had the good fortune to have the influence of many mentors in my life. Aside from my parents, Maurice Watson was my first mentor. He is an educator of the highest order. His influence on my life has been immeasurable, because he showered unconditional love upon me. He has been consistently caring in my personal life and in regard to my career, from my youth right up to the present day.

When I was sixteen, I remember listening to Francis Coppola and cinematographer Vittorio Storaro discussing filmmaking. This was a turning point of my life, for I was able to understand their passion and realize that I, too, could pursue an artistic life.

As a playwright, I now look to August Wilson for inspiration. After hearing my acceptance speech at the Tony Awards in 1992, he said to me, "I'm gonna get you a pen and some paper, 'cause you need to be writing."

My friendship with Roscoe Lee Brown is one of the great joys of my life. His gentleness, wisdom, and intelligence inspire me every day that

I live—in my humble attempts to emulate his manner, his way of speaking, his way of simply being. I find that my sense of self is much improved. It was Roscoe Lee Brown who influenced me to use my given name professionally.

The most valuable lessons I learned from my mentors are these: One, always remain openhearted and open-minded; and two, you get more flies with honey than with vinegar.

DAVID FROST

INVESTIGATE TO FIND
THE TRUTH

Only one person comes to mind who can be considered a mentor in my life—Geoff Cooksey. He was my English teacher from the time I turned fifteen until I was eighteen.

In 1956, I had just moved to a new school because my father was a minister and we traveled a lot. Mr. Cooksey was a remarkable human being whom I encountered at this very formative time of life. He ignited my interest in words as well as my passion for them. He made words irresistible to me.

One particular assignment comes to mind. Mr. Cooksey was concerned about the differences between a "loaded" article and an accurate one, between fiction and the truth. For that reason he told us to read two newspapers instead of one so we could learn to decipher this difference. We were taught to investigate in order to find the truth and not to be afraid to question what was going on or what was being said.

When the 1956 war over the Suez Canal occurred, it caused great difficulty in England. England, France, and Israel attacked Egypt after its president, Gamal Nasser, nationalized the Suez Canal. Many people opposed the actions that were being taken. In fact, this was the beginning of a great division in England between those who supported the Suez actions and those who were opposed. At this time, Mr. Cooksey had us reading the *Observer,* a Sunday newspaper, so that we could keep informed of the current situation.

We were urged to observe and to heed the great changes that were only just beginning to shape England at that time. This was occurring when it was still run by the "old school" style of rule: when leaders were more than adequately aware that they were still our—the students'—elders and our betters and that their way of operating was best and proper. Also, about this time Mr. Cooksey took us to see a play by the brilliant playwright John Osborne. The play was called *Look Back in Anger,* and it was staged at the Royal Court Theater in London. The main character was a boy called Jimmy Porter, who originated the phrase "angry young man."

This play, and Mr. Cooksey, taught me to be more aware of the outside world, to observe the changes that were now going on in the country, and to question the nature of things, particularly words. He also taught me how to relate what I was learning in English class, concerning literature and words, to the world around me. He explained that English is not just an important subject to which I must pay attention, but that the lessons I learned serve as paradigms for life experiences.

Mr. Cooksey gave me a new view of the future. He was an inspiring man who offered valuable lessons about the world. He taught me not to be afraid of change but to confront it head-on and to look past an initial impression; to question the meaning of things and to learn from the changes those close observations can bring about. His teachings were instrumental because they inspired me to think for myself. He helped me to see the sheer pleasure in words and to learn from them. And he stimulated my mind. He was my mentor and my friend.

WHOOPI GOLDBERG
ALL THE RIGHT INGREDIENTS

Belief in progress and moving forward is very important.
Even if you don't attain your goal, you should at least
realize that you have tried and that in attempting you have
achieved a great deal. Failure is not an end in itself. It is
simply a means of continuing forward.

My mother, Emma, was a great, great person. She had all the right ingredients that influenced me as I was growing up. She was a chaperone when we were taking a school field trip once. It was at a time when everyone was starting to form cliques. I wanted to be in a clique so badly. I wanted to be in a cool group. At the time of the field trip, I had just gotten in one of these groups and was very happy. However, everyone in the car was making fun of a friend of mine, but I wasn't doing anything about it. In fact, I was taking part. My mother, who was driving, stayed quiet the entire time.

After the trip, my mom noted that this friend had had a really tough day with all the kids in the car giving him such a rough time, and she was surprised that I didn't do something to help him. "I know how you hate it when people make fun of you or when people hurt your feelings. I'm surprised that you would hurt someone else's." It was like someone had hit me over the head with a baseball bat. It was a fundamental lesson that I have kept with me as years have passed and things have gotten more complex: Treat people like you want to be treated and always meet people and interact with them on an individual basis.

I was also fortunate enough to have gone to a summer camp, Madison-Felicia, for a number of years in Peekskill, New York. The camp was an extraordinary experience for me. I met people from all walks of life, many of whom remain good friends. It seems that I came into contact with the right people at the right time.

I look back at those times and those friends and see how I got to be the way I am today. I'm a composite of so many people that I have known. It's like I was a sponge absorbing them. Those friends really helped to shape me. They also offered an outlet for things going on in my life. I could share the best and the worst with them and know that they would be there for me. And I tried to be there for them as well.

Over the years, so many people have set me on this path and taught me so much. One of the most important lessons I have learned is that, as an individual, you have the capacity to achieve a goal. You have to apply yourself and, by applying, learn the ritual of trying. You may not accomplish your goal, but the idea is trying to get there. Belief in progress and moving forward is very important. Even if you don't attain your goal, you should at least realize that you have tried and that in attempting you have achieved a great deal. Failure is not an end in itself. It is simply a means of continuing forward.

I learned this lesson from my mom and my friends. I'm very grateful to them for helping me to learn this.

TIPPER GORE

DON'T NEGLECT
YOUR EDUCATION

I have always felt that it is important to revere and honor older people for their experience and wisdom. Perhaps that feeling grew from the meaningful role that my grandparents played in my upbringing. I remember most vividly my grandmother's influence and wisdom. She told countless stories about her family and upbringing. Through the telling of these stories, she taught many lessons and provided a sense of continuity to the past as we shared time in the present. She taught me her skills: cooking, sewing, gardening, and managing relationships. Whenever I had a problem I would go to her with it, and she would help me sort through the different issues. Sometimes she would just issue the solution, which was comforting in itself. I felt that she was always there for me, right or wrong, to listen and to love me.

I was raised in a religious household where personal morality mattered a lot. My grandmother helped instill in me a very strong sense of right and wrong and personal responsibility. She always told me, "Don't neglect your education. It's the one thing nobody can take from you."

Outside my family, one of my strongest lifelong interests has been the art of photography, an interest that grew from the encouragement of another mentor in my life. When my husband and I lived on a small farm fifty miles from Nashville, Jack Corn was the photo editor for the *Tennessean,* the local newspaper in Nashville. My husband had given me a camera and I began taking a photography class with Jack, driving one hundred miles round-trip to attend each session. He taught me everything, from the principles of photojournalism to printing and processing pictures. He gave me tremendous encouragement. Even more than that, he offered me a part-time job at the *Tennessean.*

I started out in the photo lab, developing film, and progressed to printing pictures, and finally to shooting them. After a while I began doing photo essays, taking the pictures and writing the text. When the paper published them, it convinced me that I could make a contribution outside the home and family, and that photography was a means to communicate about larger social issues. When the paper published my photograph of an evicted woman sitting on a curb in the rain, I was gratified. But when calls to help her flooded the newspaper, I realized the power of the photograph to communicate a human being's personal pain and that power could move people to help their fellow man.

While Jack saw photography as art, he primarily viewed it as a form of communication. Today, my love of photography, nurtured through the interest that Jack took in my work, lets me capture images of my family as well as some truly historic moments that took place during my husband's term as vice president of the United States.

CHARLES GRODIN

OUTWORK EVERYONE

The person who changed my life was my father, and so sadly for me he did it by unexpectedly dying at fifty-two. I was eighteen.

That was such a harsh blow to me, one from which I've never fully recovered, but it's made everything bad that's happened since not have the same negative effect I've seen on others. Somewhere in me there's a voice saying, "Compared to what?"

It's impossible for anyone to go through life without experiencing what sometimes feels like constant setbacks. Spending the first forty years of my professional life in show business, I've experienced and possibly seen more rejection than in any other field. Even door-to-door poetry salesmen experience less.

Because of this, most others leave show business within a couple of years. I earned about three thousand dollars a year my first ten years in the field, and I have absolutely no memory of suffering at all. I knew I was getting better, and that's all that mattered.

For the most part, my dad acted as though he didn't like me, at least from about fourteen on, because I didn't show up every day after school to work in his store. He sold supplies to cleaners, tailors, and dressmakers—things like hangers, trouser guards, linings, and eventually material to make suits. He also sold buttons.

As I recall, my main job was counting one hundred forty-four buttons, putting them in an envelope, and marking it as a gross. My dad thought I was not only shirking my responsibility to help as much as my older brother dutifully did, but also that I was downright lazy.

Of all the things anyone who has ever known me might say, lazy wouldn't appear on the list. In fact, when I told my mother I wanted to be an actor, she said, "No one makes a living in that field." I said, "I'll outwork everyone." I would never say I've outworked everyone, but I've never met anyone who outworked me—not even close—to their detriment.

Also, money was not the issue here. My dad easily could and did hire a kid for fifty cents an hour to count the buttons. He was absolutely astonished that I gave the speech as valedictorian at my high school graduation. That lazy kid!

My dad found it so difficult to talk to me about how much I worked at the store, but in spite of all our problems, I knew he loved me. I knew because more than one customer said to me on those days when I worked, "You're the one who wants to be an actor. Your dad is very proud of you."

My fondest memory of my father came when I was about ten. My mother and dad were taking a rare vacation. My brother and I saw them off at the train. My dad leaned down and kissed my cheek. That was the only time that ever happened.

I adored my father. His passing made everything else bad that's happened to me impact a lot less.

RAY HALBRITTER

MENTORING BY EXAMPLE

*As my mother demonstrated for me, the best teaching tool
is not what you say you are or what you say others should
be—it is what you are.*

To me, the fundamental task and value in mentoring lies in doing
what you want others to do. I believe that you have to live as an
example. In my life, my mother always set that example, and she continues to do so today.

One of the most remarkable things about my mother's attitude
and outlook on life is her utter lack of resentment toward those who
may have wronged her personally or Native people in general. My
people, the Oneida people, lost their homeland, despite promises in trea-
ties that our birthright—my mother's and mine—would be protected.
Before the colonists came, our people were self-sufficient, self-governing,
and living in peace with our neighbors. Their arrival basically
destroyed everything we had and took so much away from our people.

Today's Native people still live with—and, in some cases, still suf-
fer from—the effects of what happened in the past. Every tragedy,
regardless of its scale, ripples outward to some extent, and it remains a
part of your mental outlook long after the event itself is half-forgotten.
So, as a Native person, you are confronted with this dual reality, and
you have to find a way to reconcile the terrible cost to your people in
the development of the dominant society—and try to salvage the truly

good things that the dominant society does have to offer. And that is where my mother was and is truly exceptional.

My mother has told me many stories about her life as a young girl and young woman. For a few years, she worked in the city of Syracuse as a maid, cleaning houses. She would walk three miles to the boundary line of the Onondaga Indian reservation, where the bus stop was located. Then she would take the city bus to downtown Syracuse and walk from the bus stop to her job. She would spend the day cleaning people's homes, and then she would walk back to the bus stop, take the bus to the stop at the Onondaga reservation, and walk the three miles back home. She was traveling between two different worlds. In Syracuse, she worked for white people who had money. To her, they were rich; at least they were comfortable enough that they could pay someone to clean their homes. Then she would come back home to the reservation and see Indian families, including her own, living in abject poverty. Sometimes she even saw Indians inebriated on the bus ride home.

It would have been easy for her to blame the white man for the sometimes distasteful and even humiliating conditions Indians lived in, or to be embarrassed by the condition of some of the intoxicated Native people she saw around her. She did neither. What she saw as the defining difference between the lifestyle and conditions of the Indians that were her family and those of the white people she worked for was education. Successful, financially secure people were educated; thus, education was the pathway out of poverty and degradation. So, rather than growing up with resentment, bitterness, and hatred, I was constantly reminded of the value of education, for my own future and for the future of the Oneida people.

To be honest, there were times when I did not share my mother's belief in education or attitude toward the dominant society when I was younger. I struggled with my own resentment, and I was not always convinced that education would really help us change our deplorable condition. But as I grew older, I began to appreciate and understand the significance of my mother's outlook. She was not telling us to ignore injustice or to just lie down and take it. But holding people accountable for the wrongs they have done to you and giving in to anger and hatred are two different things. And being on the receiving end of great injustice is no excuse for not performing up to your potential—or for not taking advantage of the opportunities in front of you. She kept us free from the shackles of resentment, anger, and hatred, and as a result, we never used them as a crutch to justify our mistakes or our failures. And that, in itself, is no small accomplishment.

As I have gotten older, I have realized more and more that the incredible significance of my mother's mentoring lies in the example she provided for me in the way she presented herself and her life to me and to others. She continues to lead by example, and her influence has led me to try to do the same.

Many of the stories she has told me about life have gained meaning as I have gotten older, too. When she was a young girl, she knew her mother did not have much money, and she would try to help out in little ways. When she had homework, for example, she would write very lightly on the sheet of paper. She would turn it in to the teacher to get her grade, and when she got the paper back, she would take it home and erase all the work so she could use that sheet of paper again. She would do that over and over again until the piece of paper wore out.

On one level, this is a story about being poor, saving money, and making the best of the situation. But on another level, it is a story about dedication to one's education. So, in a certain way, the lesson this story taught me was about how important education was to her and her children, and to Native people.

Of course, as a leader, I cannot tell our Oneida people (or anyone else) to go get an education if I never pursued my own. But because I did go to college and law school, other Oneida people see that it can be done and that it can lead to good things. For example, one of our members came to me once and demanded a better job, stating, "I have a family and I need more money." I said, "We cannot give you a better job simply because you need one; we have to pay you what is fair for the contribution you make in your job." Then I recommended returning to school. This person started to object: "I have three children. It's too hard to go back to school when you have three children."

And then his voice began to trail off because, as he gazed into my eyes, he realized that I had five children when I obtained my undergraduate degree, and six when I went to law school. I did not even have to muster a response; the argument was made by what I had done.

In my opinion, mentoring by example is truly the most effective way to influence someone else. As my mother demonstrated for me, the best teaching tool is not what you say you are or what you say others should be—it is what you are.

PETE HAMILL
TO ERR IS HUMAN

Outside my family, there were no mentors in any conventional sense. I did have one huge role model (although that awful phrase was thankfully not in use): Jackie Robinson. His example was there for all of us. He was intense, passionate, focused. He always pushed his talent to its furthest limit. In 1947, the year he became the first black American to play in the major leagues, he was the epitome of stoic values. No matter how brutal the outside pressure might be (from racists and the media), he kept his mouth shut and played ball. If he could do that, in the face of such terrible provocation, we could, too. It's more than a half century later, the Brooklyn Dodgers are gone, and so is Jackie Robinson. But I still find myself asking, in time of personal or professional difficulty: How would Jackie handle this?

Where I grew up in Brooklyn, nobody had ever gone to college, and few had even finished high school. But while I was serving in the U.S. Navy, a number of people encouraged me to go on to get a general equivalency degree (GED) and use the GI Bill as a means of attending college. I did. At Pratt Institute, a marvelous teacher named Tom McMahon encouraged me to write. He organized a small group of us—all comrades from Brooklyn—into a reading group, and every week we focused intensely on certain classics. We read Hemingway, Fitzgerald. We spent many weeks analyzing Aristotle's *Ethics*. I'm sure that McMahon realized that we would have to understand issues of right and wrong before we could do anything with our lives. Until it was destroyed a few years ago in a fire, I carried my copy of the Penguin paperback edition of *Ethics* with me for more than forty years. It was at once a study of moral philosophy and an artifact of my youth. Once in a while, I would open it and smile at the young man who had studied it so intently; he had underlined all the wrong passages.

I became a newspaperman in 1960, working nights at the old *New York Post*. I was untrained, immensely ignorant of the craft. But some master craftsmen guided me along the way. Ed Kosner, later editor of *Newsweek, Esquire,* and *New York* magazine, helped me through some of the most difficult tasks. A copy editor named Fred McMorrow taught me much about sentences. But it was Paul Sann, then the executive editor, who most clearly fit the role of mentor. He could be corrosive when I was lousy. He could give hints of praise when I was good. He put me alongside more experienced writers so that I could learn more swiftly. He let me write multipart articles. He made me a columnist. He sent me to Vietnam and to riots and to political conventions. He even loaned me money. I suppose he was a mentor, but I thought of him as my friend.

He once told me, "If you have the story, tell it. If you don't have the story, *write* it." He urged me to read good writers and to analyze why they were good. "If you don't read, you'll never write," he said. "And if you read good writers, you have at least a chance of writing well yourself." He also warned me that the newspaper business was certain to break my heart. It did, and I didn't care. The run had been very long and very sweet.

In the end, a mentor can only move you part of the way to your goal. The mentor cannot accompany a person every hour of the day; we need guidance but not guardian angels. To get through an entire life, each of us must develop a secret mentor, hidden, private, living in our minds and imaginations. That personal mentor can be a composite of a number of people, those we know and those we have never met.

But that mentor of the self must be rigorous, stern, compassionate, just, and also have a sense of humor. We are all capable of folly; it is, alas, part of being human. And the truly great mentor—real or imagined— is also forgiving. We might, on occasion, be required to forgive our friends and our enemies, our parents and our siblings, our spouses and our lovers; the luckiest of us might never have the need to do so. But we will always have a need to forgive ourselves. If that doesn't happen, if we make no mistakes, if we are more perfect than saints, then we will not have lived a life. The hidden, secret mentor in each of us must be in charge of taking responsibility for mistakes, forgiving them, and then starting again in the morning.

One final thing: If you are a young person who cannot find a real flesh-and-blood mentor, do not despair. There are literally thousands of mentors to choose from and all of them can be found in the public library. Every library is a temple of human wisdom. On the shelves, in those books, is the tale of the world with all its villains and heroes. Choose the company of heroes. Read the *Meditations* of Marcus Aurelius. Read the letters of Seneca, *The Count of Monte Cristo*. Ride with *Don Quixote*. Sail with *Ulysses*. Hear the tales of the *Arabian Nights*. Go in and meet Albert Camus, whose father died when he was two months old. His mother could not read or write, and they lived in the grim slums of Oran in North Africa, and she never read a word her son wrote. But Camus won the Nobel Prize in Literature when he was forty-two. Don't let anyone tell you that you can't walk the streets with Albert Camus beside you. Read him. Read about Jack Roosevelt Robinson and what he did in the summer of 1947. And reach for a copy of Aristotle's *Ethics*, too. They are all waiting for your arrival.

MARCIA GAY HARDEN

I WOULD HELP YOU GET THERE

There is a great, perhaps simplistic desire to look back on my life and dissect the one moment, the one person, who changed its course forever. So I try to imagine the stages of growth, try to squint far down the alley of my past and see if—in perhaps the warm embrace of a babysitter, or in the words of a day-care teacher—someone had planted a nugget in me when I was very young. Possibly a neighbor, or someone in my elementary school, had "made me what I am today. . . ." This squinting goes on through high school and college and the early days of waiting tables and auditioning in Washington, DC, and finally takes me to New York, where even more waiting tables and audition-ing and grad school occurred. Then I squint through the early mar-riage years, and then the having-children years, right up to the present. As I open my eyes wide, I realize it's not that no one was there . . . but that no one person was there. The squint reveals many faces and gentle (or not so gentle) guiding hands. The squint reveals people who have encouraged me, who have given me ideals, led by example, enthusiasti-cally educated, and presented risk as an adventure. The squint reveals people who in their wisdom and hope let a sense of possibility prevail and used positive words to build tenacity.

The squint reveals first my parents and the enormous influence they had on me. Growing up as the middle of five children in a constantly traveling naval military family, my neighborhood *was* my family. My peers, role models, and best friends were my brother and my sisters. Our old Texan roots provided the moral ethics that were drilled into us: "Work hard to earn what you get in life," "your word is your handshake," "what you do, and how you do it, equals character," and "always have honor." That, mixed in with the various gruff military adages from my father—"pull yourself up by your bootstraps" and "discover your mission in life"—and the gifts of the home provided by my mother—artistic Ikebana flower arrangements gracing the Japanese tansu chest, the sweet notes tucked into our brown paper lunch bags, teaching us to sew our own gowns for the navy cotillions, and preparing family meals served on place mats with cloth napkins—these laid a foundation for a young girl growing up in the sixties and seventies to imagine herself as a working woman, yet also as a mother.

My oldest sister, Leslie, influenced me to love nature as she led overnight hikes along the Appalachian Trail; my sister Sheryl opened the door to community work by encouraging me to work alongside her as a JANGO (candy striper) for Naval Bethesda Hospital. My brother, Thaddeus, has given me an example of nobility and strength. He has emerged my hero, choosing life and joy in the aftermath of the tragic deaths of his children. My youngest sister, Stephanie, has shared an extraordinary sisterly generosity as she helped me prepare for motherhood.

There are people and influences at every stage that have helped lay the foundation for the next uncertain steps, some even gave me a push through the door.

There was a debate and acting teacher when I was a student in Munich, Germany, who simply said: "You are good. You have a gift."

Those words of encouragement as much as anything else gave me a nugget of direction in life. Here was something I was good at, that I had a passion for—could I actually be an actress?

There was an acting teacher at the University of Texas named Lee Abraham, who made the craft and skill of acting a wonderful discovery.

There was Zelda Fichandler, the most important woman in American regional theater and head of the graduate acting program at New York University's Tisch School of the Arts, who gave me a full scholarship, making it possible for me to attend their renowned acting program.

There was Ron Van Lieu, master acting teacher, who had such a remarkable "honesty radar" that I still seek his advice when I am developing a particularly complicated character.

There are the Coen brothers, who gave *me,* a complete unknown, fresh out of school, a starring role in their film *Miller's Crossing.* They didn't need "names"; they trusted their own vision, and as a result I had a door open in the film business for which many wait a lifetime.

But it was in 1994, while shooting the film *The Spitfire Grill,* that a really big nugget landed in my lap. I met the woman who would become my lifetime mentor, the great actress Ellen Burstyn. Her credits, her film work, her numerous Oscar wins and nominations, had me eager to work alongside her. She transformed completely into her character, she unearthed the darkness and light of each character, she worked with a concentration peppered with humor and delivered with skill. This was the actress I most wanted to emulate! But it was her life philosophy, her wisdom, her patience, and her poetry that allowed me to slowly intrude upon her privacy, so that I might steal some of her energy and strength for myself. I fairly basked in her friendship, flattered that she should take an interest in me. Picking wild asparagus at her Vermont cottage, which she had rented during the film, Ellen spoke to me of her past, of love, of personal history, and of the joys and the turbulence of life that are always invited into the human investigations of character. We were similar, she said. She stood up for me with fierce loyalty as we investigated interpretation of various scenes. Once, when I had saved my tears for my close-up, Ellen said, "Don't ever do that again. Had I seen *that* performance . . . my own would have differed vastly." "But . . . but . . . what if I didn't have any tears left for my close-up?" I asked, mortified. "How would I get there?" She answered firmly, "I would be there for you. I would help you get there."

That simple answer—"I would help you get there"—describes best what mentors can do: Simply, they help you get there. They shed light on situations that are momentarily dark, providing illumination and guidance as you find your way. Ellen doesn't believe that energy or strength is stolen but that it is shared, borrowed, expanded, until there is enough for everyone to grow. It was an important and insightful lesson that she shared with me, one that I have returned to many times since, and just one of many that she has imparted to me throughout our long friendship.

KITTY CARLISLE HART

THE VALUE OF BEING YOURSELF

I went to Hollywood to try to become a movie star, but I didn't feel that I was movie star material and also felt that no one was particularly interested in me. So I returned to New York, defeated.

Then I met Moss Hart. He was a wonderful and brilliant man. We had been married only a short time and he was working on a film that would become *Gentleman's Agreement,* with Gregory Peck. He was to finish writing the script in Hollywood. We were staying at Otto Preminger's house and going to a big Hollywood party that evening. Since I didn't do so well in my first foray into Hollywood, I was leery of going back. It frightened me because it seemed to reinforce my feelings of failure.

Before we went to the party, Moss sat me down in our room. "All your life you've been living under a cloak labeled Kitty Carlisle," he said. "And you keep the cloak over you because you feel no one wants to know who Kitty Carlisle is." He asked, "Do you know how wrong you are?" He went on to tell me that when we went to the party, he was going to leave me at the door. "If we stay with each other, we won't have anything to talk about when we get home." We went to the party, and Moss left me on my own for the entire evening. I had a wonderful time. He had proven his point.

That evening became the turning point in my life. Moss really taught me the value of being myself. He gave me the desire to remove the cloak I was hiding under and let people see me. He showed me that people were genuinely interested in me. Most of all, I gained a new sense of self-worth, and it made such a difference.

I felt that I was married to a genius, and anything he did was fine by me. We had such fun together. And such growth. Moss Hart was always an inspiration for me. I learned so many valuable lessons from him and feel blessed that we were able to share so much of our lives together. I love him very much.

JULIA BUTTERFLY HILL

THE TREE TAUGHT ME HOW TO SURVIVE

My commitment, my work, and my prayer is that we, as a human family, we, the human animal species, will remember and reconnect with the earth.

Growing up, I did not really have people in my life who were positive mentors for me. Mostly, my experiences of people showed me who I did not want to be, because I experienced a lot of violence and abuse in the home. I was physically punished for just being myself, which made me feel like I was wrong and bad all the time. It was hard growing up feeling like who I was as a person was not okay.

At the same time, my parents did teach me some very important lessons. For example, they taught me that no matter how little one has, there is always something to give. We grew up extremely poor, so when I was a very young girl, we created a program in our community where we gathered day-old food from shops and food from food banks and we would separate it into bags and pass it out from the back of a truck to people in need in our church and in our community.

I was also raised to appreciate and respect the natural world. My two brothers and I spent a lot of time playing outside, and my parents took us camping frequently. From the time I was about eight and a half years old until I was in high school, my family did not have a house and lived out of a camper trailer pulled behind our car. Oftentimes, we were in a different city every other day. Nature was my playground and also where I went to find solace and safety from the violence I experienced.

Over time, I began to realize that nature was a great teacher. If I paid attention to the sights, smells, and sounds around me, I could learn a lot from the experience. I also found that when I was angry, upset, frustrated, or sad, if I went out to nature—even if it was just a single tree growing in a square in the sidewalk in the city—and became still, I would begin to sort out what was upsetting me and begin to feel better.

When I was twenty-three years old, I found out that over ninety-seven percent of the original ancient redwoods had been logged and that of the remaining three percent, many were still being cut down with horribly destructive logging practices. As trees were there for me when I needed them growing up, I felt like I needed to be there to protect these trees. I climbed eighteen stories up into a two-hundred-foot-tall redwood tree and did not touch the ground again for over two years. This thousand-year-old elder tree became one of the greatest teachers and mentors of my life. It taught me more than I ever could have imagined learning in an entire lifetime, let alone two years.

The tree taught me how to survive the storms of life's experiences without breaking—don't be rigid, bend and flow. The tree taught me the power of unconditional love—breathe in life's toxins and transform them into healing, and that is how I will grow. A tree's growth rings are formed by breathing in our toxins and transforming them into clean air and a stable climate. It taught me that I needed to be bold in my vision and reach for the sky, and at the same time, I needed to be practical and rooted in the ground—to be grounded in the reality of the situation while reaching and stretching toward the seemingly impossible.

For me, nature always has been and always will be my greatest teacher. Other people have a lot of wisdom to offer, and I do my best to learn from every person and every experience. And yet, it is to the natural world that I go to learn and to remember the "Nature" of our "Human Nature."

My commitment, my work, and my prayer is that we, as a human family, we, the human animal species, will remember and reconnect with the earth—remembering that it is not so much *our* earth as something we own, but rather *us earth* as this sacred, living, breathing, deeply interwoven and interconnected family of which we are part. All of us are the ancestors of future generations. What do we want our legacy to be?

ANNE JACKSON

THE BEAUTY OF TEACHING

Miss Edwards was a middle-aged English teacher in junior high school, P.S. 171, who had an enormous influence on my early development. She gave me monologues to perform in assembly. I would stay after school and she would direct me in pieces such as the monologue from *Anne of Green Gables*. At this time my mother was in a mental hospital—I was only twelve or thirteen—so it was important to have this dear, caring woman in my life.

She taught me the value of sense memory (an acting technique used to emphasize emotional realism), although she didn't call it that. She simply saw memory as a facet of the power of the imagination. For instance, I would sit on a stationary chair in the classroom pretending that I was riding a horse-drawn carriage with Mr. Cuthbert, one of the characters from *Anne of Green Gables*. Miss Edwards made sure that I rocked back and forth and actually "saw" trees, "felt" breezes, and "talked with" Mr. Cuthbert.

Miss Edwards helped me realize my strength as an actress. Five years later I performed the monologue from *Anne of Green Gables* on the stage of the John Golden Theater in Chicago. This got me my first job in the road company of Anton Chekhov's *The Cherry Orchard* with Eva Le Gallienne, who was a major star of the theater in the 1940s and '50s.

She helped me to set my course, and I've been an actress ever since. I've had many kind adults, both male and female, assist me in the course of my career, but I believe that it was Miss Edwards who was most important to me.

Today, I teach actors and learn as much from them as they learn from me. That, to me, is the beauty of teaching. Helping others brings a great amount of pride and enjoyment, whether you are an adult or a child. Each of us must have the capacity to learn and continue to learn. Growth is always inspiring.

JAMES EARL JONES

SELF-RELIANCE

First of all, let me say that I don't believe in mentors. That is, I don't believe that people can set out to be role models; if they do, it is usually somewhat false, and it doesn't work. For instance, a parent can't just decide to be a role model for his or her child. When such a relationship does exist, it usually just happens, because that child sees something in his role model that he responds to positively, which helps him search within himself to find his own potential.

I was raised by my grandparents, and I would say that my grandfather was, and still is, my hero. Outside of the family, my most influential role model was a high school English teacher, Donald Crouch. Professor Crouch was a former college teacher who had worked with Robert Frost, among others. He had retired to a farm near the small Michigan town where I lived, but when he discovered that there was a need for good teachers locally, he came to teach at my small agricultural high school.

Growing up, I had a hard time speaking, because I was a stutterer and felt self-conscious. Professor Crouch discovered that I wrote poetry, a secret I was not anxious to divulge, being a typical high school boy. After learning this, he questioned me about why, if I loved words so much, couldn't I say them out loud? One day I showed him a poem I had written, and he responded to it by saying that it was too good to be my own work, that I must have copied it from someone. To prove that I hadn't plagiarized it, he wanted me to recite the poem, by heart, in front of the entire class. I did as he asked, got through it without stuttering, and from then on I had to write more and speak more. This had a tremendous effect on me, and my confidence grew as I learned to express myself comfortably out loud.

On the last day of school, we had our final class outside on the lawn, and Professor Crouch presented me with a gift—a copy of Ralph Waldo Emerson's *Self-Reliance*. This was invaluable to me because it summed up what he had taught me—self-reliance. His influence on me was so basic that it extended to all areas of my life. He is the reason I became an actor. Several years later I was in Shakespeare's *Timon of Athens* at the Yale Repertory Theater.

Of course, Professor Crouch was the one person I knew I definitely had to invite, and so I asked him to come see me. By that time, though, he was almost completely blind and said that he would rather not come if he couldn't see me. This was a disappointment, but I understood why he didn't want to come and knew that he was right. In terms of overall influence, he is still the most important person outside my family whose inspiration has helped and guided me over the years.

VAN JONES
ASK THE RIGHT QUESTIONS

The mentor who has most influenced my life is the man who was my journalism professor at the University of Tennessee at Martin: Dr. E. Jerald Ogg.

Many people know me as an African American liberal activist. They would be surprised to know that my friend, confidant, and mentor is a white conservative Republican who teaches in the Bible Belt. Despite our political differences, he recognized my talent and took me under his wing when I was his student in the 1980s. With his intelligence and multiple degrees, Ogg easily could have gone to Washington, DC, or Wall Street and made out quite well. But instead he chose to come back to his rural alma mater to give back. I'm glad he did. He has been my closest advisor for nearly twenty-five years.

Ogg gave me three pieces of advice that changed my perspective and my life. First, public institutions are equal to private ones, if you take advantage of the opportunities they offer. Second, speak your truth, even if it provokes controversy. Third, choose options that open up the most possibilities for the future.

Ogg's first piece of advice came when I was thinking about transferring from UT-Martin to Vanderbilt University. My girlfriend at the time, Monica Peek, was a student leader at Vanderbilt. I wanted to be closer to her and to graduate from a more prestigious school. Ogg advised me to stay put. He explained that UT-Martin had one of the best communications departments in the state, so I was not going to get more knowledge by spending more money. Then he pointed out that I could then springboard to any graduate program in the country—if I did exceptionally well on the campus where I already had a base of support. I stayed and participated in every program offered—student government, you name it. I did well and was then able to go on to Yale Law School.

I adopted Ogg's respect for public institutions. Even to this day, my work is about fixing big public systems—initially reforming police departments and juvenile justice systems, and later modernizing job training programs to be eco-friendly.

The second piece of advice was to trust in the democratic process. I was a crusading student editor of the campus newspaper. We covered hot topics like campus racial relations, concerns about the corporation running the student cafeteria, AIDS as a new issue, etc.

Ogg could have easily asked us to cool it. For example, AIDS prevention through condom availability is not so controversial today. But it was a lightning rod topic in the Bible Belt back then.

But he told us, "Just stick to the facts on the news pages, tell your truth as best you can on the editorial pages, and trust the campus to make sense of all this. Don't back down because some of these topics are not popular or comfortable."

I still believe in raising the tough issues. You should always reserve your right to change your mind, in light of new facts and experiences. But democracy works only when people put their opinions out there. After the fussing and fuming is over, good solutions usually emerge.

His third piece of advice helped me decide to become an attorney. During my senior year, I was accepted to numerous law schools. But I also had a job offer from the Associated Press. Should I become a reporter or a lawyer?

Ogg said: Don't just grab the best-looking short-term option. Make the choice that maximizes your life choices down the line. He explained, "When a baby is born, everyone is awestruck. No one knows what he or she will become—president, Olympic athlete, etc. There are limitless possibilities. But when you die, there are zero possibilities. So life is a process of going from infinite choices to no choices. The happiest people in the world are people who still have lots of choices. The saddest people are those who don't. So always make choices that create *more* choices—because that keeps life interesting."

In my case, the AP offer was tempting: I could have worked in Nashville close to my girlfriend and gotten a paycheck. But I concluded that an attorney can easily become a reporter later on. But a reporter cannot easily become an attorney later on. Therefore, I chose law school. I graduated in 1993 and focused on public advocacy—which combines legal and media work.

I still seek choice-maximizing opportunities for learning and growth. Quite famously, I went from being a national advocate for green jobs to serving briefly in government. There was some risk because my activist past was pretty colorful. But I decided to answer the call to serve. I learned a ton, and any pain was greatly outweighed by my gain.

Ogg has watched my rough edges get shorn off—sometimes more painfully than others. But he has always been there, even counseling me when my father died.

I couldn't have been successful without Ogg's mentorship. No matter how talented you are, you are really the summation of the coaching you get. The best athlete in the world can still get beaten by a competitor who has a better coach.

I still call Ogg "The Coach." He never tried to give me the right answers; instead he gave me the right questions to ask. That's the true role of a mentor.

LARRY KING
TRUST YOUR INSTINCTS

My mentors taught me to never be afraid to take a risk,
never cop out on my values, never lie to a friend, and above
all, that all things will pass.

When I was a child, all I wanted to do was be on the radio, and there were two great radio broadcasters who influenced me and whom I admired. Arthur Godfrey was a wonderful broadcaster who exemplified great values—he was a risk taker, had a great personality, and above all, he was always himself. Red Barber was a Dodgers announcer whom I not only listened to as a child but also tried to imitate. I can remember pretending to be him when I was about ten years old, doing imaginary sports broadcasts by myself. I later met and worked with both these men, which was like living out a dream.

Both of these men had an enormous influence on my career as a radio broadcaster, for they taught me several important lessons. From them, I learned to be myself and to take risks. They showed me that in our profession the only secret is that there is no secret, and that above all I should trust my instincts. They gave me simple advice—to be the best I could be.

On a personal level, there were several people who had a tremendous effect on my life. Mario Cuomo, through his brilliance and friendship, taught me the importance of having a strong character. One of my favorite people has been Stan Musial, a baseball player.

However, one individual who had an enormous influence on me was Edward Bennett Williams, a genius in the courtroom and a wonderful friend and adviser. Just being in his presence had a strong effect on me. Above all, he exemplified truthfulness and taught me that it was no shame to show one's feelings.

There is one moment I shared with Edward that has stayed with me. I was walking with him down Connecticut Avenue two weeks before he died of cancer, and he knew he was going to die. He was cheering me up, telling me what a great career I had and what a wonderful life. I asked him, "Aren't you scared?"

He was a devout Catholic, had always gone to church regularly, and he replied that if this life was all there was, then it didn't make any sense and everything was just one big cosmic joke. Why do anything, he asked. Why work? In his mind, there had to be something greater than our life on earth, and he accepted this calmly. This concept was much more logical to him than the idea that there was nothing. I'm an agnostic, and his words had a tremendous impact on me. I can still hear his voice, saying those words.

Another great friend, whom I have known since we were nine, is Herb Cohen. Herbie taught me that you can negotiate anything. He would get me in trouble and then get me out of it again. When we were seventeen years old, we were walking one night when a squad car pulled up next to us. The police began questioning both of us about a series of robberies that had recently occurred, for we fit the description of the robbers. I immediately started to cry; Herbie, on the other hand, confessed to the crimes. He thought it would be fun to take a trip to the police station. He was crazy then and is still crazy now, and I consider him my closest friend.

Paul Newman told me once that anyone who had gotten anywhere and doesn't acknowledge the influence of luck is fooling himself. I was lucky enough to be born with some talent, and I had the ability to pursue my dream, but much of my success can only be attributed to luck. However, the influence of the friends and advisers I have had throughout the years has strengthened and helped me along the way.

From the relationships I have had with these men, I have seen that circumstances change but that people never do. You don't lie to your friends, for friendship is one of the most valuable things you can have. One is lucky to have even one good friend, and I have been lucky enough to have three or four, Herb being the closest.

The fact that all of these role models, both personal and professional, were outside of my immediate family made a great difference in my life. My father died when I was nine and a half, and so an older male influence was very important to me. I was raised by a strong loving mother and had a younger brother, but these key people outside of my family gave me support of a different kind.

The four men I have mentioned had a collective impact on me, teaching several important lessons through their examples or their friendship. They taught me to never be afraid to take a risk, never cop out on my values, never lie to a friend, and above all, that all things will pass. I am a commentator, not a brain surgeon. I do not save people's lives. Knowing that I am not more important than anyone else, that I go on the air at nine o'clock and then off again at ten really puts things in perspective. This kind of awareness is important to anyone who has risen to prominence in their chosen career, for falling down can be much harder than rising up.

EDWARD I. KOCH
THE CARDINAL AND ME

Many people have profoundly affected my life, but the person who comes to mind first is the former Archbishop and Catholic prelate of New York City, John Cardinal O'Connor.

In 1986, during the third term of my mayoralty, a scandal erupted in New York City's Parking Violations Bureau. The corruption involved Queens Borough President Donald Manes and Bronx Democratic Leader Stanley Friedman, neither of whom was appointed by me. Both were independently elected and used their power to corrupt the Bureau, stealing hundreds of thousands of dollars, perhaps millions, from the people of New York City. Fortunately, the conspiracy was detected during a taped police telephone conversation involving organized crime in Chicago.

While I was in no way involved with the corruption, the scandal happened on my watch and was devastating to me. Although I didn't realize it at the time, I believe the shock left me clinically depressed.

During those trying days, the most comforting call that I received was from John Cardinal O'Connor. He phoned me at Gracie Mansion (the mayor's residence) one Sunday morning to say he knew I was depressed and that I shouldn't be. "Everyone," he said, "knows you are an honest man." When I thanked him, he said, "Don't thank me, it's true." I replied, "Your Eminence, you called me, the Lubavitcher Rebbe did not call."

The cardinal and I were great friends before and after that incident. Indeed, we wrote a book together in 1989 entitled *His Eminence and Hizzoner*. As a result of his call, I began to recover my bearings, and the psychic pain that made it difficult for me to function went away. The memory of his kindness and his willingness to reach out to me and comfort me when he knew I was suffering will never fade.

Nevertheless, the cardinal and I never hesitated to argue with one another privately and publicly regarding public issues of the day. Indeed, we often clashed. One such conflict involved a mayoral executive order that I issued prohibiting discrimination on the basis of sexual orientation, meaning that homosexuals and lesbians could not be banned from employment in agencies providing services under a city contract. The Catholic Church superbly rendered many such services. The cardinal sued the City of New York, stating that the Church did not ban homosexuals or lesbians from employment, but under existing law it, along with all religious institutions, was exempt from such an order. He won that lawsuit.

When Archbishop O'Connor was to be ordained a cardinal in Rome by Pope John Paul II, he asked me to join a group of five hundred New Yorkers traveling to Rome for the ceremony. I was delighted to attend. At a dinner that evening, he referred to me and our friendship saying, "Only in New York can two people who are such good friends sue one another so often." I loved him then, and I think of him often.

I have been invited to attend Midnight Mass at St. Patrick's Cathedral by Cardinals Cooke, O'Connor, and Egan, and I have done so for more than thirty-five years. Before the mass begins, the cardinal usually acknowledges some of those in attendance. On two occasions, John Cardinal O'Connor made my night with his introductions. Once, addressing the crowd, he said, "Mayor Koch is in his seat. Let the Mass begin." On another occasion he said, "There are three thousand people in the Cathedral tonight, many of whom are not Catholic. If you feel uncomfortable not knowing what to do, just look in the direction of Mayor Koch and do what he does."

Have no doubts or expectations concerning me and my faith. I was born a Jew and shall die a Jew. I am fiercely proud of my faith and religious tradition and have rejoiced in and defended it all my life. I also rejoice in and defend the faith of Catholics as well. I have treasured my friendships with their cardinals, princes of the church, who have enriched my life.

In the 1989 Democratic Primary, I lost my bid for a fourth mayoral term to David Dinkins. After my concession statement, I returned to Gracie Mansion with many friends and family members. At midnight there was a knock on the door. It was Cardinal O'Connor, who embraced me and said, "We will stay in touch with one another." And we did.

In 2000, when the cardinal was suffering from cancer, the priests who had graduated with him from the seminary so many years before went to his home to celebrate his birthday. I went to his residence as well and gave him a sculpture of the Madonna's head taken from Michelangelo's Pieta, which I knew would delight him, and it did. In his agony awaiting death, he joked and made everyone around him comfortable.

John O'Connor was a special person, anointed by God to comfort everyone with whom he came in contact. I was privileged to be one whose life he touched. I keep the remembrance card of his funeral at St. Patrick's Cathedral on my desk, and when I occasionally look at his photo, I am comforted once again.

Dr. Mathilde Krim
An Anchor in My Life

I was one of those lucky children who grew up in a nurturing, cohesive, and extended—almost clannish—family, which included two parents, four grandparents, and many other relatives. And yet, I always yearned to explore beyond the family circle because I felt a need to break out and compare members of my family to others. I did experience the important and positive help of mentors, but only starting in my teens and young adult years.

One of my mentors was a stern and demanding but inspiring Latin and history teacher. In two years of high school, he taught me the disciplines of logical thinking and writing. To date, I remember Mr. Chevalier's words and face, his demeanor and smile, and his ability to inspire intellectual delight. He also helped me find relieving humor in the course of stern lectures. There was also a female English teacher whom we, in an all-girls high school, dreaded, but whose love of English literature was so winning and contagious that I came to love and admire her greatly. These two individuals taught me a lot about setting personal standards of performance. And being able to live up to the expectations of such individuals greatly helped my self-esteem in my teenage years.

Throughout the years, various mentors have entered my life for short or extended periods of time. Some have been older friends, teachers, or senior professional colleagues. They all have broadened the frame of reference provided by my original family, and they have helped me to compare notes, to assent or argue with them, and in total to think for myself, break out of a preordained mold, and find my own way in society.

What they all had in common was that they were freely chosen by me to be attentive, respectful of me, and older. Each in one way or another was an anchor at some time in my life, somebody whom I could hold on to in case of need, who would listen to me and respond honestly. In that sense, each was a true mentor.

EVELYN H. LAUDER
FINDING GUIDANCE

It's terribly difficult to name just one person who has most changed my life. First, there's my mother, whose resolve to flee to the United States when the German army, under the leadership of Adolf Hitler, annexed Austria, not only saved most of our family but also saved my parents' lives and my own.

Then there's my father, Ernest Hausner, who was most erudite. He was a terrific geographer and political analyst and, at an early age, taught me to keep connected with and informed of issues of the day (something I certainly didn't appreciate at the time). He also insisted that I learn the metric system, even though it wasn't regularly taught in US schools.

My husband's mother, Estée Lauder, was a terrific mentor. A woman of extreme ambition, determination, passion, and punctuality (which never transferred to me), her response to any situation was always, "Let's get it done yesterday." Don't think that didn't rub off on me!

Another mentor, whom I've known for over fifty years, is, of course, my husband, Leonard Lauder. He has nurtured all my ambitions to succeed in our business so we could have parallel lives and schedules. He has always made time for me—as he has done for so many others—to advise, guide, and encourage. He listened to and found valuable my ideas and gave me a sense of empowerment and influence as a result of the implementation of those suggestions. He, like both my parents and in-laws before, is fiercely loyal, loving, and close to family and is, above all, my dearest friend.

MAYA LIN

STRONG INFLUENCES

My brother and I grew up in Athens, Ohio, where my parents worked as professors at Ohio University. They had recently immigrated from China, which isolated us from the community but which also created a unique closeness within our family.

I learned a lot from my mother and father, perhaps more than other children do from their parents. In China there is an emphasis on the family serving as the primary mentors. This was certainly true for my family.

Each member of my family has been a creative influence. My father was a ceramist, my mother is a writer, my brother a poet. Our closeness as a family seemed to fuel our own artistic natures—we are always learning from and inspired by one another. My approach to architecture was very much influenced by my father's methods as a ceramist. When making models I frequently use a material called plasticine. It is a claylike substance that does not dry or harden and allows me to continuously mold and shape the material. It is a direct influence from my father.

I was very fortunate in my early education. From the first to sixth grades I went to a school where the student-teacher ratio was very much in the favor of the students. There was one teacher for every twelve or thirteen children, allowing the teachers to address the needs of each student on a personal basis. My art and chemistry teachers are individuals I still keep in touch with today.

I have had two great teachers in my education at Yale University. Professor Vincent Scully was a critical influence on my thoughts of architecture as a social and personal practice. I studied under him as an undergraduate, also serving as a teacher's assistant while I was in graduate school. Professor Scully really directed my thoughts on the way architecture shapes how we feel and experience a place. I began questioning how my work would affect people. How would people feel when they saw my work? What was I trying to express to them? These became key questions I ask in my approach to each project. I would begin at the end, understanding the effect I was hoping to convey, and work to develop the technical means to produce this effect.

Frank Gehry, a visiting professor at the graduate school of architecture, was also a very strong influence on my work. He was the only person who told me not to worry about whether I was an artist or an architect, telling me that my work crossed over boundaries and that I shouldn't worry about the distinctions. It was advice that has helped me pursue a course that places me between the fields of art and architecture.

I am very lucky to have been influenced by my family as well as my teachers. My family has always been there for me, educating me artistically and personally. My teachers helped push me to think and view my work in various contexts. I would not be where I am today without them.

SIRIO MACCIONI
STICK TO YOUR CONVICTIONS

My father and mother were Italians from Tuscany who died during World War II. After their deaths my sister and I went to live with my grandmother, Nunzia, who stressed simplicity as a worthy goal in life. She was an intelligent woman who wanted us to do the best we could. "Don't wait," she would say. "Do something now." She tried to create my character early and wanted people to feel at ease around us. From her I learned to be socially correct and proper. She must have foreseen my future line of work.

When I was seventeen, I had the opportunity to go to France. Once there I was helped a great deal by a fellow Italian who was also from Tuscany—the famous singer and actor Yves Montand. He was an extremely talented man, a man of conviction. He was also a very controversial figure at the time and accused of many things. He was even labeled a Communist because he went to Russia as a performer. But he also helped me in my early days in the restaurant industry. He helped me to survive in Paris by finding a job for me in a restaurant. I am very thankful to have known him.

If you wanted to work in the restaurant industry in Europe, it was necessary to know several languages. Being in Paris, I had learned French, but I still needed German, so I moved to Germany and lived there long enough to learn the language. Then I had the chance to go to America.

I came to New York in 1956 after working on a luxury cruise liner as a waiter and dancer. I could not speak English, but someone helped me a great deal. Oscar Delmonico gave me my first job in New York and was instrumental in helping me enroll in a six-month English course at Hunter College. I was going to school during the day and working in the restaurant at night. It was not the steadiest of jobs—I was mainly a replacement when other employees could not come in—but it helped me with the bills.

I received my green card in 1958 and began working at the Colony Restaurant on 61st Street in Manhattan, which was owned by the Cavalerro family. Soon I realized I knew all the customers. I had met many of them when I was working in Europe, and now I could speak whatever language they spoke; I was very qualified. I was soon promoted to be the temporary head of the Colony and was written up in *Life* magazine.

In 1974, with the help of the Zeckendorf family, who managed the Mayfair Hotel on East 65th Street, I opened a new restaurant called Le Cirque. Mr. Zeckendorf took a chance with me because he believed in me. I ran Le Cirque from 1974 until June 1996, then I moved to the Villard Houses on 455 Madison Avenue and reopened the restaurant as Le Cirque 2000 on May 1, 1997.

I would like to thank all the people who have helped me in my work. I have met all of the most important people in the United States and many world leaders. I knew President Kennedy and his parents. I think he was a nice man and a good president. My family and I were shocked when he was killed. I also knew President Nixon personally. He was nice to my family and even advised my sons about their college education, especially since I really did not know much about colleges and universities.

Of all the things I have learned, one of the most important is to have an open mind and respect people, but stick to your convictions.

I have a great wife. She was a famous singer in Italy and also had a show at Carnegie Hall in New York. Together we have three sons: Mario, Marco, and Mauro. We all speak three languages fluently. They all went to good schools; I made sure that they had a great education. I wanted a doctor, lawyer, or a president—but they all work with me selling soup.

My dream in life is to have a good home and a good family. My work has been successful, and I have been able to be at home in Tuscany and New York. My entire family meets in Italy as often as we can, but always in summer. I have fulfilled this dream. I just always want to be together with my family and, of course, have great food.

HOWARD S. MAIER
TEAMWORK AND MOTIVATION
ACHIEVE SUCCESS

Sam Stryker was my first "boss" at Clairol. He taught me motivational marketing skills that enabled me to eventually become a successful entrepreneur. Sam emphasized the importance of teamwork and motivation to achieve success. This proved to work for me, both in the corporate world and as an entrepreneur.

The division of labor in large business organizations is vast and very detail oriented. Sam Stryker saw the need to get employees to respond to the needs of the organization in which they worked. The trick of leadership lies in motivating employees to perform specific tasks that, along with the tasks of others, combine to form the finished product of that business.

Sam believed it was important to turn people on to your project. You also had to know how to turn a negative situation into a positive result. He knew the importance of positive motivation. His philosophy of a business's success paralleled that of Sam Walton: You emulate what people do well and try to change what they don't do well. You try to improve on their particular drawbacks and then attempt to transform them into strengths.

One way to achieve this result lay in training. Although marketing is an art, one must still learn basic skills. Sam took the time to train me in marketing operations as well as employee motivation.

Another key component of Stryker's philosophy was to put the company above the individual. Again, this is part of his teamwork mentality. Sam believed in the value of camaraderie inside and outside the office as a strengthening agent for the business itself. He saw this as relevant to dealing with people and motivating them. The statement "It's not me, it's we" has also become a valuable standard for me. In my business, I have always viewed my success as *our* success. I, too, incorporate this belief, whether I am sending parents a baby gift or taking employees to a New York Knicks game. People will respond to you much better if they feel you care about them.

PETER MAX

EIGHT THOUSAND YEARS
OF INFLUENCE

When I was young, I didn't want to be a painter. I spent my first ten years in Shanghai, China, and the country itself served as my first mentor. I was this small Caucasian boy, an only child, surrounded by this amazing eight-thousand-year-old Oriental influence.

I became fascinated with the holy people of Shanghai. I would see Buddhist monks on my way to school every morning. You would look in their eyes and just see an ocean of calm. I also got to know the street artists. They were like monks in the way they renounced the material things of the world. They lived on the streets of the city and created beautiful art. I saw Buddhist sand paintings for the first time in Shanghai and am still fascinated by them today.

The street artists inspired me, and I started drawing and painting as a child in China. I had a nanny, Uma, who would draw with me in the garden surrounding three-quarters of my family's three-tiered pagoda house. She taught me to hold my brush in the Oriental way. Uma also bought me these small colorful posters illustrated with traditional Chinese stories. I loved the intricate color arrangements found in these different art forms. Their influence would later show up in my work.

Being an only child, I was also enormously influenced by my parents. I remember walking with my father to the store one day and seeing a street vendor sitting on an orange crate. He had small bundles of what appeared to be newspapers. Upon closer inspection, they turned out to be American comic books. My dad bought these bundles for me, and for the next several weeks, I devoured them. I loved the outlines of the comic books, the sense of geometry and borders, and their color schemes. Quite unknowingly, I related color to a sense of atmosphere, of mood, that relayed the themes of the stories. Somehow all this clicked with comics.

Comics led to a fascination with American movies. I remember the first time I heard the word *director* and asked what it meant. It was then that I made the connection that this magical stuff in the movies was from someone's mind. It was a creation. It was someone's story.

All this Americana, including jazz, was like seeds that would slowly germinate for me. When my family moved to Brooklyn in 1953, I became fascinated with astronomy in high school. I loved the concepts of space and stars existing light-years away. I loved the concept of infinity. I thought I would be an astronomer. I was excellent at math and really lucky with several teachers who encouraged my enthusiasm. At the same time, I continued drawing and painting. I started drawing stars and then began with some of the monks I had seen in China. My parents were so supportive of me. My mom made the biggest fuss over anything I did, and my peers were supportive as well. This made me work twice as hard.

Over the years I found my own style and visual ways to tell my own stories. I strive to do just that. But I wouldn't be where I am today without the life I have led so far and the various influences I have had.

SENATOR
JOHN MCCAIN
MOORINGS AND A COMPASS

A former high school teacher of mine, William Ravenel, changed my life. I was the son of a naval officer who led a transient life. When I was at a boys' boarding school of mostly southern well-off families, Mr. Ravenel gave me some moorings and a compass. He was a man of such admirable qualities. He had been a football player at Duke, he'd been in World War II in General Patton's tank-core, he still served in the Army Reserve, and he was a coach of a junior varsity team that I was on. Believe it or not, he made Shakespeare come alive. He used his classroom as not only a way to teach English, but also to teach values, and standards, and morals.

Mr. Ravenel was so admirable you wanted to be like him. And it wasn't just me, but the other boys as well. Even though this was a boys' boarding school, he realized that with a certain humility and seized the advantage to impart on us the honor code that was part of the school there and the teaching of the various classics. He somehow imparted not just the telling of them, but the meaning of them. That had a great impact.

I discussed all manner of subjects with him, from sports to the stories of Somerset Maugham, from his combat experiences to my future. He was one of the few people at school to whom I confided that I was bound for the Academy and a navy career, and to whom I confided my reservations about my destiny.

One instance in particular stands out in my memory as a moment when Mr. Ravenel's support really boosted my confidence. Training rules were a part of the honor code that you signed and agreed to observe. In the fall of my senior year, a member of the junior varsity football team had broken training and faced expulsion from the team. Mr. Ravenel called a team meeting during which players argued that the accused be dropped from the team and referred to the honor council. I didn't think that was fair. Since the student in question had, unlike the rest of us, chosen at the start of the year not to sign a pledge promising to abide by the training rules faithfully, I argued in favor of a less severe punishment.

Most of my teammates wanted to hang the guy. But I argued that since he had not been caught breaking training but instead had confessed the offense and expressed his remorse freely, his behavior was no less honorable than that of a student who signed the pledge and adhered to its provisions. My defense swayed the people in the room, about twenty or thirty guys. Mr. Ravenel closed the discussion by voicing support for my judgment.

After the meeting broke up, Mr. Ravenel approached me and shook my hand. With relief evident in his voice, he told me we had done the right thing and thanked me for my efforts. He allowed that before the meeting he had been anxious about its outcome. He had hoped the matter would be resolved as it had been but was uncertain it would. Still, he had not wanted to be the one who argued for exoneration; he wanted the decision to be ours and not his. He said he was proud of me. That was very important to me.

I have never forgotten the confidence his praise gave me. Nor did I ever forget the man who praised me. Years later, during the time I was imprisoned in Vietnam, I thought about Mr. Ravenel a lot. He was the one who reinforced in me the standards of honorable behavior. I was faced with several decisions and one in particular, would I accept an offer of the Vietnamese to go home early? I thought about the fact that Mr. Ravenel had been in combat in World War II and thus had a feel for what I was involved in. And I really believed, at that time as I thought about it and considered it, that Mr. Ravenel wouldn't look favorably upon such a decision, because it was not an honorable one. So, I refused the offer. Most important, although I am sure that Mr. Ravenel had his failings, I never saw them. I idolized him. I wanted to be like him.

After I returned home, Mr. Ravenel was the only person outside of my family that I wanted to see, because his approval or disapproval of me was probably more important than that of anyone else in my life, besides my father. I felt he was someone to whom I could explain what happened to me, and who would understand. That is a high tribute to Mr. Ravenel. I regret that I was never able to pay him that tribute. Upon my return I found that my mentor had passed on. Mr. Ravenel had died of a heart attack two years before my release from prison. He lived for only fifty-three years. His early death was a great loss to his family, friends, and students, and to everyone who had been blessed with his company, a loss I found difficult to accept.

Were William B. Ravenel the only person I remember from high school, I would credit those days as among the best of my life. He was an inspirational man, and I wasn't the only one that he inspired. His influence over my life, while perhaps not apparent to most who have observed its progress, was more important and more benevolent than that of any other person save members of my family.

I think that a mentor can help you through difficult periods, help you see the difference between right and wrong. The world is more complicated for children today than it ever was when I was growing up. A mentor can provide you with the kind of an idealism that you can look up to and attempt to emulate. What I believe young people find very useful is someone that they can contact and interact with, and frankly express their doubts and their concerns and their questions. We have found through scientific study that a mentor can dramatically impact a young person's life. I knew that Mr. Ravenel had a great impact on me. But I don't think I really understood how deeply he impacted me until I was in prison; it was his example I looked to when I was tempted to do something that was less than honorable.

MIDORI

THINK FOR YOURSELF

*A house needs to be built on a solid foundation. A
foundation of sand does not hold. An artist also needs a
foundation based on sound thinking in order to be inspired
and for that inspiration to be a success.*

There were people who inspired and encouraged me by their
thoughts and actions in my personal as well as my public life.
Perhaps some of them did not exactly fit the bill of mentor in the sense
of being a teacher, but they exerted a strong influence—they supported, encouraged, and consoled me, and they still do so today.

Two of them are my closest friends. Two others are great artists—
one living, the other now gone. One taught me that if I believe in
something, I must act on it: Take the initiative and do not wait for others. Be involved; be active.

The other artist challenged me constantly and made me realize
how important it is to think for myself and bear responsibility for what
I do musically. He questioned everything and opened my eyes to
what was possible. When you are a soloist, you must be fully aware
of why you do what you do. Of course, music is deeply personal, but
when you produce music without thinking, it is not your music. Your
musical and artistic potential is not realized. Some musicians will dis-
agree here on the theory that artistic merit springs from spontaneity, and

in a way it does. We remember Thomas Edison's remark that "invention is ninety-nine percent perspiration and one percent inspiration."

I believe that inspiration comes to you only after you understand the logic of what works and what does not. A house needs to be built on a solid foundation. A foundation of sand does not hold. An artist also needs a foundation based on sound thinking in order to be inspired and for that inspiration to be a success.

Now, about my two friends. I've known them both for a long time. One is a wonderful role model: She believes in herself and in what she does. On a daily basis, she reaches for the best within herself to give to her work and to others. She is always, always motivated to solve problems and achieve goals. She participates in life to her fullest capacity and shares herself generously with others.

My other close friend influenced me in a different way. He helped me to discover myself and to learn what was meaningful and truly important. In a busy world with demands from without and within, sometimes our inner feelings are left unheeded. This man was available to me, without an agenda of his own, when I most needed someone. He defined friendship and trust for me.

In terms of inspiration, I am revitalized again and again by the children I meet through my work with Midori & Friends. They allow me to share what I love, and they accept whatever I offer. Our process of engaging is primal, personal, and valuable to me. It is always a pleasure and an honor to share what I have. Indeed, it is a privilege.

These people shaped my life. I cherish the inspiration they have given to me and to my work and am grateful that our paths have crossed.

ANN MOORE

SEIZE THE MOMENT

We should all be mentors just like Governor Richards and
Jackie Joyner-Kersee because that is the smart thing to do
with our time and our money.

I was very lucky in my life to be adopted by a mentor. One day in my fifties, this wise, irreverent force of nature with perfect comedic timing and a silver helmet head of hair showed up on my sofa. Governor Ann Richards from the great state of Texas announced she was here because she read I was the first female CEO of Time Inc. and she had come to teach me how to play at the varsity level.

Ann had moved to New York City after 9/11. That was just like her to barge in as others were fleeing. Ann Richards believed gender is an issue for politicians, for CEOs. No day passed in her lifetime, she once told me, when she wasn't keenly aware that she was a female. There was no day without a "you Tarzan, me Jane moment," but she rejoiced in the differences.

The governor couldn't understand people who were not politically active, who didn't vote. She thought government and business worked better when women leaders were present. (She was right, by the way.) So it was no surprise to me that she worked hard to establish a school in Texas to train girls in leadership. As I look around my circle of women friends, I am in awe of how many recognize this need to mentor.

A *New York Times* reporter interviewed my friend Jackie Joyner-Kersee in Barcelona. She was staying with me on the *Sports Illustrated* ship since her asthma didn't do well in non-air-conditioned athlete dorms. The reporter was speculating that Jackie would be retiring soon.

Jackie said, "One day."

"What will you do?" asked the reporter.

"I'm going back to East St. Louis to open a community center for kids."

"Really?" said the skeptical reporter.

"For how long?"

"FOR THE REST OF MY LIFE!" barked my friend Jackie.

We all may need to commit to public education and closing the dangerous gap between the haves and have-nots for the rest of our lives. We should all be mentors just like Governor Richards and Jackie Joyner-Kersee because that is the smart thing to do with our time and our money.

One of Time Inc.'s newest magazines, *Real Simple,* ran an editor's note a few years ago that reminded me of another reason, too. It was a rabbi's advice at a wedding ceremony to a new bride and groom: "If you want to be happy for an hour . . . take a nap," said the rabbi. "If you want to be happy for a day . . . go fishing. If you want to be happy for a week, go on a honeymoon. If you want to be happy for a year . . . inherit a fortune. But if you want to be happy for a lifetime . . . help other people."

I made a contribution to the Ann Richards School for Young Women Leaders in Austin, Texas, and to the JJK Boys & Girls Club in East St. Louis because there is simply no better way to pay forward all that Ann Richards did for me. Every single year she would end the *Fortune* Most Powerful Women Summit by reminding us all to keep our sense of humor, to simplify our lives, to give up on perfection, and to take responsibility for our health. "The here and now is all we have, and if we play it right, it's all we'll need. Seize the moment."

JOSIE NATORI

EVEN MY GRANDMOTHER'S LAST RITES DID NOT KEEP HER DOWN

I was the first of thirty-three grandchildren and spent most of my summers with my grandmother, Josefa Almeda, in the province of Camarines Sur, in the Philippines. My grandmother was an amazing woman entrepreneur. She owned and operated businesses ranging from ice manufacturing plants and drugstores to movie theaters and plantations. She was a hands-on businesswoman. As a child, I would spend my days riding in a Jeep around Naga City and its outskirts with my grandmother as she visited her businesses. We would rise at five o'clock in the morning and not stop until midnight. To me she seemed like the mayor of the town, traveling and holding court.

She was a strong woman—the mother of eight—who always stressed the importance of independence to me. She believed that women, even married, should have their own means of support and never have to depend on anyone or anything. She also believed that individuals controlled their own destiny. She was the personification of all she preached, which made quite an impression on me.

She taught me the value of self-discipline and the continuing need for self-improvement and education. I was always learning something, whether it was a foreign language, cooking, typing, or the arts. Her energy was my inspiration. She never stopped, and early on I decided to be as much like her as I could.

My grandmother was voracious about life. She said that you can't just talk about things you wanted to do, you had to act. Words were never enough for her. It was all about action, being tough on yourself and giving your all. She never complained, and she lived every minute of life to the fullest. Within her lifetime, I think she must have traveled to about one hundred countries.

Even in her last years, she didn't let her battle with cancer get in her way. After a prolonged battle with the disease, she received the sacrament of last rites on her supposed deathbed. Everyone thought she was gone. I called her long distance and told her that she needed to get well so we could travel again. Miraculously, she improved and managed to travel to New York to spend time with me before we set out for a two-month tour of France and Spain. Every day her strength seemed to improve. All this after receiving last rites!

I think she knew that this was her last journey, but even then she refused to slow down. She died at eighty-nine, having lived life to the fullest more than anyone I have ever known. I feel blessed to have experienced it with her firsthand. To others she must have seemed a force of nature, which she was.

Another person from a completely opposite sphere that I feel blessed to have known was my piano tutor, Olga Stroumillo. I had taken piano lessons from the time I was four, but I really didn't appreciate the beauty of music until I began studying with Madame Stroumillo. She was Russian, a best friend of Vladimir Horowitz and, earlier in her career, an assistant to Sergei Rachmaninoff.

She was a very philosophical woman. She always told me that everything in life, like everything in music, is connected. To her, music was simply a metaphor for life itself, for the act of living. "Nothing is an accident," she would tell me. "One thing leads to another like fingers on the keys, like notes within the scales. Music is life."

Like my grandmother, Madame Stroumillo preached the need for self-discipline and being tough on yourself. She also spoke of the truth found within music and within yourself. To create something beautiful—in music or in life—you have to approach it from a place of truth. Truth is essential to both.

Madame Stroumillo lived her last years using a walker, barely able to care for herself. However, her brother was in much worse physical condition, and she was determined to move in with him.

When I pointed out her own ailing health, she responded with a smile that she had to care for both of them. She was determined to live longer than her brother because if she died first, he would have no one else. She did outlive him.

Both of these women were immensely important role models. They approached life with a sense of purpose and self-sufficiency and amazed people with their own acts of willpower and survival. I feel blessed to have had their encouragement and belief in me. I was always in awe of them. They enriched my life so that I feel they are still with me.

JESSYE NORMAN
KIND WORDS

I feel very fortunate that I can think of many adults in my childhood who were influential and caring, and who offered counsel and support. My public school teachers figure prominently in this group, particularly my second-grade teacher, who invited me to sing before the entire student body when she noticed my enthusiasm for music. Of course I was thrilled. It was a large school with hundreds of students, and I felt very proud since my parents attended the school program where I sang. I was a heroine for a day—in my own classroom. It is still a wonderful memory. I feel a certain degree of confidence was acquired quite painlessly and naturally.

Other important influences came from the adults in my community and church. It was an era when adults did not hesitate to correct the behavior of children not their own, because they felt the parents would agree with them completely.

As my mentors changed with my own maturation, I cannot point to just one person and say that this individual affected my life in a major way. My high school chemistry teacher propelled my interest in science and medicine, which remains with me. My junior high school music teacher made sure that I continued voice studies. She played piano for me all over my hometown of Augusta, Georgia, and many other places in the area. And we learned songs together. She remained a valued friend.

All of my mentors were equally important. The love and care that came from growing up in a small community enabled me to find them everywhere and in many different situations. Every kind word and every act of support reminds me that I was very lucky and that it is my responsibility to express the care that I received.

ROSIE O'DONNELL

MARAVEL

ms maravel—a twenty-something beautiful
almost hippie math teacher
who was engaged to mr pic—
the band teacher i loved instantly

she—ms maravel—
caught me in the hall
without a pass
the third day of seventh grade

"open your locker—take out all the books"
I did—speechless
with arms full she slammed the locker door closed
"next time—detention, now go"
and I did
our first meeting
without even a hello

pat maravel died last week
nearly three decades after our rocky start
we buried her today
i sat today in the front row
where she placed me from the start
inside her family
a part of, my very own

i was born twice—
once in 1962
to a woman who left so quickly,
i never got to know her
i carry her name
and from the few photos i have
her face as well

i was born again
in 1975 to pat maravel
a woman who refused to let go

she forced life back into my soul—
she stood solid and strong—
she showed up—
she stayed

i never got to ask her why she did it
rescued this lost puppy of a girl
motherless and starving
nothing special in any way

what did she see in me?

i tested her for years
not able to trust—still so broken
but i couldn't shake her
no matter how i tried
and i did
i was her most difficult child
she always says—
said
past tense
it hurts to breathe

will i ever stop referencing my mother
i feel like liza—with a z
here we go again
this old chestnut

when my mom was sick
i thought if barbra's mom was sick
she would go on johnny carson
and ask people to send a dollar
and she would buy medicine
and her mom would live

i believed that true
it's not

i have the money now
and my second mom was not saved
there is no magic medicine

"do you think i am dying?"
she asked me in december
"yes" i answered
"me too" she said

then after a moment,
"ro, this is going to be very hard for you"
i laughed as i cried, telling her
"i could not love you more—
i will look after the two you pushed out"
she put on her glasses to get one last look
held my face in her hands
and said "now go"
i did

god has a sense of humor
she gave me two mothers
both died of breast cancer
both times i am devastated beyond words

pat maravel taught me about mothering—
freedom and family
about tolerance—activism and compassion
she showed me how to live—how to love—
how to give back
she had strong opinions with an open mind
and a will to live that defied doctors' rules

i watched myself on 20/20
talking about parenting
i realized just today
i sounded like pat
the way i speak to my children
is the way she spoke to me

when she was dying—
almost too ill to talk
i brought an eight by ten of the kids
for her to see
she smiled with the parts of her face
that still worked

i put it on top of the dresser
in plain view—near the window
after an hour of only one-word replies
i got up to go

she stared at me hard
wanting to say something
i could tell
she nodded toward the picture

"the photo, teach?"
yes she nodded
i took it down and brought it to her
all emotional and dramatic
"did you want to see the kids, pat?"
she rolled her eyes at me and said
no—window
then laughed

my picture was blocking her view
of the birds and trees
i got it—cracked up
then retold it to joy, dolores, and jessie
in front of her
she laughed every time
her closing joke

i miss her a lot
now especially
when i feel so much like myself
again

barbara walters asked me if my mom
would be proud of me

she was—
her name was pat maravel
she told me so

DR. MEHMET OZ
WORK HARD, WORK SMART

I have two role models. That's important because I'm a Gemini and I always need to have balance but also opposing forces in my life, whether it's me creating them or getting them from different folks.

My father and father-in-law, both renowned surgeons, were colleagues and respected each other but were very different people in how they lived their lives and what were their perceptions on life. They weren't partners but they saw beauty in each other, and I learned from both of them.

My father grew up in a poverty-stricken part of Turkey in 1925. He left Turkey to come to a country where he didn't speak the language. He knew how to take chances. He was never given anything. As a result, he was always overprepared for any eventuality. He took on any challenge. He was a tough street fighter.

My father-in-law grew up on Staten Island, also without affluence, but did have a lot of the opportunities that America afforded a young man born in 1936. Because he was not fighting just to get an education like my father, he was able to dedicate some of his life to thinking about the role of the spirit.

I'm a bit like my father in that I can get into a tough situation and fight my way out. Like my father I thrive on work. But my father always had difficulty looking up from the maze he was running in. That's reflective of his personality. He could never afford to sit back and take the luxury of time to just "be." He had to always "do."

On the other end, my father-in-law was much more willing in any situation to not force a decision but force insight. He helped me make peace with the important realities of life, being a better father and better husband, and developing a deep-seated passion for living a life with the right goals rather than just living a life to succeed.

Work hard. Work smart. My father was a person of action. From him, I learned to trust my gut, make a decision, and move on it. From my father-in-law, I learned the passion of service and that our greatest natural resource is our ingenuity and innovation.

It's because of my father that I became a successful heart surgeon. It's because of my father-in-law that I became a successful teacher. And what I do in television is a result of both.

COLIN POWELL
THE MEASURE OF A MAN

When I was a boy growing up in the South Bronx, my father was the dominant figure in my life. A Jamaican immigrant like my mother, who worked his way up to a foreman's job in Manhattan's garment district, Luther Powell never let his race or station affect his sense of self. West Indians like him had come to this country with nothing.

Every morning they got on the subway, worked like dogs all day, got home at eight at night, supported their families, and educated their children. If they could do that, how dare anyone think they were less than anybody's equal? That was Pop's attitude, and it became mine, too. At home, my father was the neighborhood Solomon—the village wise man people came to for advice, for domestic arbitration, or for help in getting a job. He would bring home clothes, seconds and irregulars, and end bolts of fabric from the company where he worked and sell them at wholesale or give them to anybody in need.

He was totally unimpressed by rank, place, or ceremony. Once, when I was a colonel stationed in Fort Campbell, Kentucky, I invited my parents to join us for Thanksgiving dinner. My father talked with generals as if he had known generals all his life and then table-hopped through the mess hall, like Omar Bradley mixing with the troops before an invasion. I was struck by his total aplomb: Luther Powell belonged wherever Luther Powell happened to be. He was a short man, just five feet two inches tall; but like Napoleon, he was masterful.

TONY RANDALL
YOU HAVE SOMETHING TO OFFER

When I was beginning my career, my mentor was Charles Warburton, an old-time actor who had performed with such notable people as Ellen Terry and who had seen Sir Henry Irving perform. He was a mine of recollections. I loved listening to his stories about all the people he had known and the great actors he had seen. During the last twenty-five years of his life, he directed a radio show called *My True Story,* and he frequently gave me roles.

One day, he asked me to stay after rehearsal and said, "I don't know what you want to do with your life, but you have something to offer this business." Those words really struck a chord in me, because his outlook on acting was different from any I had heard before. He didn't talk about success and he didn't tell me that acting was something I should do for myself. Instead, he presented it as something I could do for others. He will always have a place in my heart for making acting something that was larger than me, something important to all people.

The man who taught me how to act was Sanford Meisner. He served as a mentor because he became the father figure in my life. I received very little emotional support from my own family, so his guidance was crucial. I studied with him for two years, and he really helped me learn the business.

Both of these men played key roles in my life, not only because they were mentors to me as an actor but because they taught me lessons about life.

CHRISTOPHER
REEVE
DECIDE WHAT YOU WANT

When I think back to my childhood, I don't recall any single individual who shaped my future. Instead, I benefitted from the influence of a number of adults, in my family, at school, and in the theater.

My parents separated when I was not quite four years old, and when I was six my mother remarried. My stepfather was a successful stockbroker who already had four children from a previous marriage, but he was more than willing to take on the responsibility of the two young boys who came along with his new wife. My father, an academic, had also remarried and soon had three more children with my stepmother. I spent much of my childhood shuttling back and forth between the two families.

The two households could not possibly have been more different. In my father's house there were always writers and musicians. By the time I was seven, I had asked my mother for piano lessons, which I continued to take through my freshman year at college.

My father was also very athletic. In the winters he took his family skiing in Vermont, and in the summers we all crowded aboard his twenty-two-foot sailboat. Because my father made these activities so enjoyable, they became an important part of my life, lasting all the way into adulthood.

But there was one difficult aspect of the time I spent with my father: He was a perfectionist who was often intolerant of even simple mistakes. I put intense pressure on myself to avoid his disapproval. Even though I often failed, I think I learned a valuable lesson, which I tried to keep in mind in bringing up my own children: Challenge them, but never set them up for failure.

The atmosphere in my other family was quite chaotic by comparison. My stepfather had to work long hours, even on weekends, to meet all his financial obligations. But he was tremendously generous. His philosophy seemed to be: Provide children with opportunities and let them learn by trial and error. As long as each child behaved responsibly, he was a cheerleader on the sidelines. When one of his eight young charges ran into difficulty, he stepped in and became a coach.

I was given a tremendous amount of freedom at a young age and became fascinated with the theater. Soon I was playing leads in plays at school as well as working backstage, and eventually onstage, with the highly regarded McCarter Theatre Repertory Company.

At the McCarter Theatre I had my first formal experience of mentoring. The artistic director was Arthur Lithgow, father of the actor John Lithgow. During one performance, I was horsing around backstage when I found myself face-to-face with Arthur. I remember him chastising me for playing such an immature game instead of preparing for my entrance. But then he said something I will never forget: "You may be the one in a thousand who succeeds in the theater. You'd better decide what you want, because you'll probably get it." In an instant I realized that it is a privilege to appear onstage and that while it may be fun to fool around occasionally, fun is nothing compared to the satisfaction of doing something well. I believe my entire approach to being an actor was formed at that moment.

I also believe that my successes have resulted primarily from this unusual combination of early influences. I had learned independence but also self-discipline. I'm not sure that either my father or my step-father realized the profound effect that each had on my development. They were mentors without even knowing it. Later in life I would come in contact with excellent teachers and fellows who inspired me with their talent. It is only because I was given so much freedom and so many privileges as a child that I was able to make the most of the opportunities that were to come my way.

LEONARD RIGGIO

LIVE BY THE COURAGE
OF YOUR CONVICTIONS

I am fortunate to have had three great mentors, each of whom had a profound impact on my life: my father, Steve Riggio; my coworker and friend Hamilton Dolly; and my first and only boss, Al Zavelle.

Steve Riggio was one of seven children who grew up in a tightly knit Italian-American family in Little Italy in Manhattan. He was a brilliant man and a great athlete. Eventually, he became a highly ranked prizefighter, whose claim to fame was that he twice defeated Rocky Graziano, who had never been beaten twice before.

Dad did not like to lose any more than he liked to get hit. After eighty-five professional fights, he left the ring without a scar on his face, and unlike most prizefighters, he never slurred his words. He remained handsome and brilliantly articulate for the rest of his life. He viewed boxing as both a science and an art, studying and practicing like no one else in the game. He won because he outboxed and outtrained his opponents. The power of his will was amazing.

Dad was completely focused on the relationship between mind and body, believing that the health of one would improve the health of the other. He drew his strength from his brain and nourished his mind from the underpinnings of a sound body. Even later, when he became a cab driver, he would always work out. At traffic lights, he would get out of the cab and do deep knee bends and push-ups. Other cabbies thought he was crazy, but they never told him to his face.

I played a lot of sports growing up and was usually the best kid on the block or on the team at most things I played. Much of this was due to the countless hours I spent at practice and the hustle I brought to the game. To this extent, I was a model of Dad's beliefs: I was dedicated, focused, and relentless.

Surprisingly for a boxer, Dad believed in weight training for most sports. He was thirty years ahead of his time in thinking that baseball players and golfers should lift weights. Back in the early 1950s, he also preached to my grandmother about working out. He was convinced that senior citizens could extend their life expectancy and add to their self-esteem with a simple fitness routine. To this extent, he was the consummate optimist. His enthusiasm and energy inspired everyone he met.

Steve Riggio also believed that a sound and active mind needed work and practice. He worked his mind as hard as he did his body. He never felt that people were born smarter than he was, and he easily made up the environmental deficiencies through his lifelong curiosity and intuition. Although Dad never graduated from high school, he completed the *New York Times* crossword puzzle nearly every day. "The pen is mightier than the sword," he would say. "Wars are nothing more than the battles over different ideas."

But to him, mentoring was not making his children into clones of himself. He gave me the resolve to live by the courage of my own convictions, not his beliefs. He rarely tried to rein me in, preferring to let me develop my own set of values and navigational system. The only thing he ever offered, which was close to an admonition, was this: "There is nothing in this world you can't do, and nothing in this universe you can't become, if you put your mind to it." He would also qualify this advice a bit and say, "Hitch your wagon to a star and you'll never land short of the moon." For those who later described me as having "humble beginnings," they never met my dad and mentor, Steve Riggio.

High aspirations and indomitable will were also the attributes of my mentor, friend, and coworker Hamilton Dolly. More than any other person before or since, Hamilton opened my eyes to the bigger world around me, purging forever my provincial inclinations and encouraging, even exhorting, me to fulfill my own destiny.

Growing up in Brooklyn during the McCarthy era, I was colored with ignorant misconceptions and outright paranoia. Just years removed from the greatest atrocities in the history of the world, the fires of prejudice burned ever brightly in America. Union activists were considered Communists; Jews were viewed with suspicion and distrust; and African Americans were treated as second-class citizens. Although Dad was a brilliant and compassionate man, his own worldview was shaped by his limited exposure; he could not, alone, expose me to the next level I so sorely needed.

Working alongside Hamilton Dolly at the New York University bookstore, I was literally bombarded with conflicting and hopelessly complex points of view. Nothing in my past provided context for the issues I needed to resolve. During these formative years, Hamilton was my mentor and my beacon. He was, without a doubt, the most brilliant person I ever encountered. His mind was as fit, as hard, and as facile as Dad's considerable physique.

As the manager of the textbook department, Hamilton took it upon himself to conduct a character-building school for the young people he supervised. He believed, as Dad did, that indefatigable effort could overcome environmental shortcomings. He lived and taught by what for him was a necessary principle. "It's *not* who you know, but *what* you know and what you *do* that creates success." He thought people should be connected to themselves before worrying about "connecting" to other people.

Hamilton always did, and continues to, believe that good work is its own reward. He instilled pride and dignity and purpose in hundreds of people, largely from minority groups, that he trained. He was a role model in providing an example of how to act, but he was a brilliant mentor in teaching people how to think.

The NYU bookstore also provided me with Al Zavelle, my first and only boss. "Mr. Zavelle" was the very first symbol of authority that I encountered in the real world outside of my home, but fortunately for me, he represented the high-mindedness necessary to be a great leader. He taught me what he knew by example and explanation. To this day, he continues to write me useful notes and kind words of encouragement. To him mentoring is clearly a lifetime commitment.

Understanding the importance of rationalizing the intersections between responsibility and authority, he took the work of managing a bookstore more seriously. In fact, he was the first college bookstore manager in America to whom the title of director was conferred, because he made the business of selling textbooks to college students an all-encompassing mission. Not satisfied with being just another administrator, he considered himself part of the faculty, and his role as critical in the process of education. To him I owe the concept of bringing missionary zeal to the workplace.

Over the course of his life, Al Zavelle always broke the mold, because he was never satisfied with the status quo. Back in the days when computers were a primitive technology, he oversaw the complete automation of the NYU bookstore's elaborate inventory management system, a feat that would not be duplicated for five years after we were up and running. A study in self-improvement, he earned his MBA in night school while working as bookstore director during the day. Naturally, he was a straight-A student, because the man simply would not accept mediocrity in anything he ever attempted.

On one occasion, as Mr. Zavelle was conducting a tour of the school supply section I managed, he came to a spot on the shelves where a certain brand of typing paper used to sit.

"What's that?" he said.

"That's the 409-IP," I replied. "It's on order."

At this point, he pointed to the empty space angrily and said, "I don't give a damn about what is on order. Our students can't type their homework on your excuses."

Although this stinging retribution spoiled my otherwise pleasant day, I have prospered since by remembering its message: Excuses are often the fine line between successful people and those who are victims of their own lack of resolve.

To this day, our college bookstore company, which now consists of more than three hundred stores, operates under this single admonition, thanks to the genius of Al Zavelle: "Cover thy shelves."

Steve Riggio, Hamilton Dolly, and Al Zavelle were three historic figures in my life and three great mentors. My life was clearly nourished by what they contributed, and their lives were to some extent enriched by what I have achieved. Mentoring is all about the nurturing relationship between mentor and the mentored: each growing because of the other. Although there can be a profound difference between mentors and heroes, some individuals embody the greatness of both.

CHITA RIVERA

NEVER STOP

We're a tapestry of every person and every experience in our lives. If you're a chorus kid, you can learn from the star; but if you're a star, you learn from the chorus kids.

I actually learned much later in life that Mother would have loved to dance. She had five kids instead and was very happy with that but had the most beautiful legs and was a most gentle and graceful person. She was the first to recognize something in me, and for her wisdom I am grateful.

She sent me to a school in Washington, DC, where I was born, run by an extremely wonderful and gifted black woman, Doris Jones, who ran the Jones-Hayward School of Ballet. Being an energetic youngster, I would probably have been all over the place if not for the focus she taught me.

You can't put your finger on what makes a gifted teacher, but it exists in the room. Her classroom was morally a wonderful place to be. She insisted on discipline and put the fear in us to achieve, but she also taught us giving, caring, and kindness to other people around you.

She was the one that really trained me not just in dance but in my life. I would take classes every day after school and weekends, and that was where I was, at age fifteen, when George Balanchine sent out some scouts from the School of American Ballet. When I was selected to go to New York to audition, I did not really understand the magnitude of dancing for Mr. B.

I remember Ms. Jones took me by the hand, and coming out of a small elevator in the building at 59th and Madison, I saw another kind of world. My class in DC was very diverse, mostly black and Hispanic, and suddenly I was in a hall teeming with a bevy of blond pony-tailed dancers and listening to screaming from the studio of the great master teacher Oboukof putting the fear of God in his students. I became very scared and nervous, and Ms. Jones calmed me with a piece of advice: "Conchita, stay in your lane. Don't worry about the beautiful long-limbed girls lining up next to you for the auditions; be who you are!" I never forgot it.

Here I was a young girl on scholarship with my nose pressed against the window watching all the greats—Allegra Kent, Jacques d'Amboise, Maria Tallchief, Edward Villella. I was nothing, but I carried the rules of respect that Ms. Jones taught me—respect for myself, for my fellow performers, and for the stage, which is sacred. "You're not out there by yourself, you can't do it by yourself, it doesn't work by yourself," she would tell us.

Years later, when I invited her to see me at the Kennedy Center, she declined. "Are you disappointed in me?" I asked. "Not at all. I don't have to come and see you. I know who you've become," she told me. She was on to training and building character for other children.

When I transitioned to the Broadway stage, it was a new kind of challenge. Peter Gennaro choreographed all of the Sharks (gang) work in *West Side Story*. He exposed me to a new kind of speed and intricate dance movement. He taught me something my spirit knew but never was allowed to do. What I didn't know, I did by feeling it.

Then there was Jerome Robbins, who I call "Big Daddy." He taught a lot to all of us about who we were and what we could do and gave us the range to explore. He would question us about our past during rehearsals and say, go home, think about it. He really taught us about the acting and the people we were portraying, and in the process, helped us to understand a bit more about ourselves. Even when the unpleasant things were exposed, these hard lessons were tools to help us grow.

There's a reason careers begin in the corps de ballet or the chorus, because that's where you learn to share the stage and learn from other people. I tell the young kids that so many fabulous teachers, choreographers, and songwriters I've worked with in my career have taught me to not be fearful and to try new things and take risks. That's how I learned who I am.

We're a tapestry of every person and every experience in our lives. If you're a chorus kid, you can learn from the star; but if you're a star, you learn from the chorus kids. I don't know what a star is, except celestial. Never stop wanting to learn. That's the most exciting thing.

ROBIN ROBERTS

RIPPLE EFFECT

The person who influenced me most was someone I never met. Her name is Wilma Schnegg. Miss Schnegg was my mother's enrichment teacher in elementary school in Akron, Ohio. In those days, the schools had teachers on staff to go beyond the three Rs and expose kids to music, arts, literature, and other higher pursuits. She changed the course of my mother's life—and because of this, changed the course of mine.

Lucimarian Tolliver Roberts came from very humble beginnings. When Mom was in high school, she got a call from Miss Schnegg, who checked in with her from time to time. At that point, Mom hadn't even considered college. My grandmother and grandfather dropped out in fifth and sixth grades respectively. It's not that they weren't supportive, but they just didn't have the know-how to get her on the college track or to even think it was a possibility.

Miss Schnegg told her about the *Akron Beacon Journal* scholarship and encouraged her to write an essay. When she won, it was announced in the local newspaper. The scholarship allowed her to attend Howard University. The day she left for Washington, DC, was the first time she had ever been on a train.

That intervention broke the cycle for my mother and my family. At Howard, she met my father and went on to live a remarkable life. She ended up getting her degree in psychology. Her first job was as a social worker in a child-welfare setting. She also worked in education for many years during my childhood.

She traveled with my dad, a Tuskegee Airman; taught all over the world; was on the Mississippi State Board of Education and the Mississippi Power Board of Directors; was a commissioner for the Mississippi Coast Coliseum; and was chairwoman of the New Orleans Branch of the Federal Reserve Bank of Atlanta. After living all over the world, they purchased a home in Pass Christian, Mississippi, where my mother continues to live to this day. There my parents raised four children—all of whom have at least a bachelor's degree.

That's the great thing about one-to-one mentoring. There's a ripple effect. When you reach out to one person, you're changing the course of not only that person's life, but their children and their children's children—and on and on. Even more than the scholarship, it's someone believing in you, believing you have a future.

I have had wonderful people in my life—bosses, teachers, coaches—but when I really think about the person who influenced my life the most, it was that person in my mom's life so long ago. It all goes back to Wilma Schnegg.

AL ROKER
ALWAYS BE YOURSELF

My dad laid the groundwork for who I am today. When I was a kid, he worked as a bus driver for NYC Transit in Brooklyn, but his dream was to become a dispatcher. He eventually became dispatcher and chief dispatcher and continued pretty far up the management ranks in labor relations, working alongside such top leaders as TWU president Mike Quill.

He was always a hustler, always working more than one job, always moving forward to achieve. I remember he ran a lunchroom out of the depot, worked extra shifts, doing whatever he could to make money and put food on the table. His work ethic started young. My grandfather was absent early and my dad left high school to take care of my grandmother and his two younger sisters. His talent was in art, but at that time there were no jobs for gifted African American artists in the commercial unions, so he got a job driving a bus.

It was a great thrill for me when there was no school to go to the depot for the day with my dad. Other bus drivers bought me ice cream, candy, comic books, and I got to ride the bus for eight hours, have lunch at Bernie's Luncheonette, and wander around the depot and see buses up on lifts and subway cars in the shop for maintenance. There was a whole group of city workers—black, white, Asian, Hispanic—who were able to achieve that American dream due to hard work and the support of their union.

In my professional life, I would have to say my mentor is Willard Scott. He's like a second father to me. In fact, had my father not died, they would have been the same age. He had two girls, and I think he looks at me like the son he didn't have.

In Washington, DC, circa 1970s, Willard Scott was the only more famous resident than the president. When we met in 1976, he was working for WRC, the top-rated ABC station in the market. I was starting my career at WTTG, the Metromedia station, now Fox, doing the weather on the ten o'clock news.

Maybe a month after I started in DC, I got a phone call and it was Willard. "Come on, we're going to dinner." I'll never forget him pulling up in this bright red Cadillac and suggesting we go for a drive. He did a U-turn in front of my television station and parked the car at this restaurant right across street, Alfredo's La Trattoria. We had dinner, and that began a mentoring relationship and a friendship that have gone on about 35 years.

Like my dad, Willard was another example of a hard worker. He was the first Ronald McDonald and played characters including Bozo the Clown. In college, he created a radio show with his roommate, a guy named Ed Walker. Called the Joy Boys, they dominated DC radio for many years with their comedy and skits. He lived on a working farm in Delaplane, Virginia. Even after he started working in television, he did birthday parties out of the farm for viewers and even sold eggs at the local department store, Higby's. He just did it all.

He was an announcer at WRC when the regular weather guy went home sick, and he got the slot until heading to the network spot on the *Today* show. After many years as a powerhouse talent, he decided to slow up and for whatever reasons recommended to management that they might name me his replacement. By then I was in the New York market at the local NBC station, and he said to me, "It's not that they're going to listen to me, but I just wanted you to have it and I told them." You're not going to find a lot of people generous enough to do that. I always said I got the job because I could wear Willard's pants and his toupee.

One of the best pieces of professional advice he gave me, that can also translate to your private life, is to always be yourself. I learned this truth from Willard because at the end of the day, that's all you got. Willard is the epitome of what you see is what you get. He's no different off the air than he is on. Truly there's never been anyone like him on television.

TIM RUSSERT

ONE GENERATION STANDS ON THE LAST GENERATION'S SHOULDERS

The most important thing my mentors did for me was to not only teach me to read and write, but to distinguish right from wrong.

In seventh grade at St. Bonaventure School in Buffalo, New York, Sister Mary Lucille, a Sister of Mercy, was both impressed and yet concerned by—shall we say—my excessive energy in class. She expressed that in her words, "We have to channel that energy, Timothy," because I was prone to mischief. One day she told me, "I'm going to start a school newspaper, and you're going to be the editor. This means that you have to give out assignments, you have to edit the copy, you have to write your own articles, you have to go around and interview students, teachers, and administrative people, and publish the paper. You have to distribute it. You have to decide whether you're going to charge for it, or if you're going to have a fund-raiser to underwrite the cost." It became this extraordinary project that I threw myself into and so did all my friends. It left us little time to get in trouble because we were so devoted to the paper, called *The Bonette* after St. Bonaventure School. Then she said, "If you don't keep up your grades we're not going to be able to do the second edition of the newspaper." That made us all committed to studying harder. It became a real class project.

On November 22, 1963, President Kennedy was assassinated. We did a special edition of the paper and sent a copy to the new president, President Johnson; to Mrs. Jacqueline Kennedy; and to Robert Kennedy, the attorney general. Some months later we received personal responses from all of them, which changed our lives. Here we were only months ago with nothing and wondering whether or not school was worth our while—whether school could be fun, whether school was meaningful—and along came this young nun who created this entity called a school newspaper that we became deeply involved in. We learned how to report, how to communicate, how to write; and then, on top of all that, people we watched on television, people who were so far removed from our ordinary lives, suddenly acknowledged not only our existence but our work. From that day forward I was determined that I would have a career in journalism/public service. I never underestimated again my ability to write, and I realized that the United States of America, no matter where you come from, no matter how distant it may be in your mind from the power and prestige of Washington, DC, you can reach it, you can penetrate it, you can achieve it through hard work and determination. And those lessons from that little seventh-grade class at St. Bonaventure School helped to form who I try to be every Sunday morning.

We continued our newspaper in eighth grade. I was going on to high school and Sister Lucille suggested I go to Canisius High School, the Jesuit school in Buffalo. I said, "Sister, it's downtown, where all the rich kids go, sons of doctors and lawyers." My dad was a truck driver and left school in tenth grade to fight in World War II. The irony is that he drove a newspaper delivery truck for the *Buffalo News,* and he delivered newspapers to the steps of Canisius High School. The notion that his son would ever go to this school was far removed. Sister Lucille insisted that I take the entrance exam, which I did. I won a partial scholarship that helped with the tuition, because we couldn't afford it. The first day when I walked in and sat down, Mr. Paul Nochelski, a Jesuit, said, "Take out a piece of paper and describe what you saw entering this building on your first day of high school." And so began Chapter Two—looking, observing, being aware of your surroundings, and trying to find a way to describe them in a way that was understandable and meaningful to other people. He opened up a new dimension just like that.

The person who would become most important to me at Canisius High School was Father John Sturm, the Prefect of Discipline. He was a former Golden Gloves boxer who entered the Jesuits, and he was tough. He would focus on the few kids who came from the south side of the city—there was only a handful of us from South Buffalo. Once when I got in trouble I said, "Father, don't you have any mercy?" He grabbed me and replied, "Russert, mercy's for God. I deliver justice." I remember it like it was yesterday. Although I knew how to write, how to report, how to observe, I learned that unless one has discipline, all of it can be lost, and Father Sturm taught me discipline.

So now I have created the Sister Mary Lucille/Father Sturm Award, a cash prize that is provided to a Buffalo Catholic school teacher each year who has made a difference in a child's life by acting as a mentor. I started this three years ago, and a thousand people come to the dinner. Every school nominates one teacher and explains what they've done for and meant to the kids. Many of the students who go to the Catholic schools in the inner city are not Catholic, but these schools give the kids a chance to become successful academically, and also teach discipline.

When I gave out the first award, both Sister Mary Lucille and Father Sturm were there. I announced that the most important thing about my education came from my two mentors here with us tonight, Sister Mary Lucille and Father John Sturm. I continued by saying that the most important thing my mentors did for me was to not only teach me to read and write, but to distinguish right from wrong. I thank them for the rest of my life for this lesson, and I hope this award will be an incentive for other teachers to understand how important it is to be a mentor in someone's life—to put kids on a path so they, too, will learn these vital things.

On Sunday mornings there's not a time that I don't think of Sister Lucille and Father Sturm. I also think of the training I received in government with Daniel Patrick Moynihan and Mario Cuomo, the training I received from the Jesuits, and the training I received in law school. In all of these areas it goes back to the same lessons—preparation and discipline. Preparation and discipline. Reading. Writing. Right from wrong. These are the lessons of life. Sister Lucille and her newspaper. Canisius High School. John Carroll University. Cleveland-Marshall College of Law. Washington and Albany. NBC. They're all building blocks. One generation stands on the last generation's shoulders. Now my son is going to have opportunities that I never dreamt of. He has met Sister Lucille and Father Sturm, and he knows the role they played in my life. There is no substitute for it—none.

In addition to this award, I've created internships at *Meet the Press,* where college students from around the country come and spend a semester working on the program, learning how to do research and how to organize their thought processes, debating the issues, studying the news, and analyzing public policy. I hope that I am training the next moderator of *Meet the Press.* The students get academic credit if approved by their college or university. Each semester we select five or six interns. I also serve on the Board of Directors for the Washington Boys and Girls Clubs, where for seven years I've been the emcee of the largest fund-raising dinner we hold annually. We raise about one million dollars each year with which we build new clubhouses for the Boys and Girls Clubs, buy computers, and provide programs for kids to come after school to do their homework with mentors and tutors, have a snack, and play sports. The success rate is unbelievable for participants in our Boys and Girls program who then finish high school and go on to college. I'm also on the Board of Directors of Colin Powell's America's Promise. So my two largest charities or activities are directly related to youth because that is our future. I know that if I had not had the intervention and support of Sister Lucille and Father Sturm I would not be the moderator of *Meet the Press*. That's my story, and I'm sticking with it.

DIANE SAWYER
BE HONEST WITH YOURSELF

*The most valuable lesson I've learned from my mentors has
been to be honest with yourself, so that you can think
clearly about what really matters: others.*

Isn't it strange how mentors arrive unexpectedly? Sometimes from
completely different corners of your psychological and geographical
world? Sometimes, complete strangers. After all, family comments—
and directives—come freighted with so much history and tender
nerves. Too intense. Too much seems to be riding on their opinions.

I don't have a single turning point—just hundreds of small ones.
Add them together and they are a road, a path. And often it's the
shock of the unvarnished truth from an outsider that can blast you like
a jet stream from one path onto another. I first learned this from the
news director in Louisville, Kentucky, who taught me the power of a
brave, blunt question. From the day I started as a rookie at WLKY-TV
in Louisville, he believed I could do it and treated me like someone
who deserved direct compliments and direct criticism. (Even when I
fell into a river trying to film my first story.)

I think next of Don Hewitt, the executive producer of *60 Minutes*,
who said once, "I love you. I *hate* that piece." It was thrilling to be
knocked down and affirmed at the same time. It almost felt like praise
and reminded me that criticism can wake you up—when it's backed by
support.

And finally, a new friend once took a big chance and said to me, "You are dying in that relationship. I'm not saying get out. But choose. Is this what you choose?" It was a seed planted. Not an instruction, but the perfect and brave comment of someone who really cared and became a beloved mentor.

So, the most valuable lesson I've learned from my mentors has been to be honest with yourself, so that you can think clearly about what really matters: others. My mentors were like wonderful mirrors— reflecting what *is,* but in a soft light. It's not that my mentors changed the course of my career or my life—they showed me the way to change myself. And that was vitally important.

Every one of my mentors has made me more confident by treating me as if I could grow. I think that's a gift to give someone at any age— including in their fifties.

ALAN SCHWARTZ

GIVING YOUR ALL
IS THE WINNING SCORE

When I was 18 years old, I faced an enviable but excruciating choice. I could sign a contract with the Washington Senators baseball team and pursue my lifelong dream of being a major league pitcher. Or, I could accept a scholarship to college, potentially slowing down my baseball ambitions but strengthening the odds of achieving my parents' goal of seeing their children graduate from college. At that time, I was fortunate to meet the baseball coach at Duke University, Tom Butters.

It's hard to describe how emotionally vulnerable young aspiring athletes are, underneath their swagger, and I was no exception. Like most of the coaches I met at the time, Tom Butters offered to refine my skills as a player. But on some level I sensed that, more important, this was a man who was even more interested in seeing me develop as a human being. I learned an enormous amount from Coach Butters, as much from observing his actions as listening to his words. He was a ferocious competitor but he made it abundantly clear that any victory attained by cutting corners was more ignominious than any defeat. And, while I shared his passion for winning, I found it comforting to know that he valued the person more than he valued the performance. "You can take 70 percent of 100 or 100 percent of 70, the answer's the same but the man is different."

As I moved into the business world, my coach's voice remained hardwired into my brain. Facing difficult decisions, I would envision having to explain to him why my choices were appropriate and that I was treating people with the respect they deserved. With the help of that filter, I knew I might not always succeed but I could always hold my head high. As the business issues became more complex, the principles remained the same, and I have always been grateful that I had Coach Butters in my life to make those lessons a part of who I am.

MARTIN SHEEN

WHEN THE STUDENT IS READY, THE TEACHER WILL APPEAR

"When the student is ready, the teacher will appear" is an old cliché that was certainly fulfilled in my life by three very different mentors who seemed to materialize at the most opportune times when I was young and most receptive. Although they could not have been more diverse in personality and background, they could not have been more alike at the core of their character or the depth of their humanity.

All three were white males—two were middle class, one was very poor—and each of their young lives had been profoundly formed by the Great Depression of the 1930s. Two were Jewish from the urban East, and one was Roman Catholic from the Midwest. Despite great family hardships and personal tragedy early on, none of them confronted life as a problem to be solved; on the contrary, each had accepted his life as a wonderful and mysterious gift to be cherished and explored. Along with varying levels of education and an abundance of natural social skills, each had developed a disciplined commitment to personal growth and service to others, and equally important, each had a unique sense of humor. Above all, as if by design, each one seemed to have developed his own deeply personal spirituality that revealed itself in compassion.

In order of appearance in my life they were: Rev. Alfred Drapp, assistant pastor at Holy Trinity Parish and School in Dayton, Ohio; Julian Beck, cofounder and director of the Living Theatre in New York; and Joseph Papp, the founder and director of the New York Shakespeare Festival and the New York Public Theater.

Father Al arrived at Holy Trinity for his first parish assignment when I was fourteen. He was an energetic young man with an innate wisdom who believed our personal relationships were reflective of our relationship to God. It was not long before he was having a noticeable effect on every family in the parish despite his lifelong struggle with shyness, which endeared him to us all the more. I served mass for him regularly, and he was my confessor.

Even as a boy I dreamed of going to New York after high school to pursue an acting career, but my father was determined that I attend college. A deformed left shoulder at birth made me, in my father's eyes, incapable of earning a living as a laborer. Hence the necessity of a higher education. This became the most contentious issue between us for a number of years. Unfortunately, I was never a good student, and when I flunked out of high school in my senior year, my father was disappointed and angry. Father Al advised me to go to summer school and graduate. He also suggested that to appease my father I agree to take the entrance exams to the University of Dayton. I did both.

Unknown to anyone, I purposely failed the exam, scoring just three percent out of a possible one hundred. My father got the message but still would not bless my dream. Perhaps he wanted to see some proof of my talent or determination. Father Al stepped forward again, and careful not to offend my father, he loaned me enough money, out of his own pocket, to get started, and soon I was on my way. Several months later, when I was settled in New York building a life for myself in the theater, my father very lovingly came around and became my biggest supporter.

Over the years my relationship with Father Al matured and his friendship became invaluable. Although my journey took me far away and at times I became lost, he was always there like an anchor reminding me to continually ask those two key little questions: Who are you? Why are you here? As long as I can answer at least one of them, I always know where I'm going, and Father Al will always remain with me.

I began working at the Living Theatre in December 1959, and for the next two and a half years my formation as an actor and a human being were greatly enhanced under the tutelage of Julian Beck, cofounder of this remarkable avant-garde and politically active repertory company at 14th Street and Sixth Avenue in New York City.

It was here that I made my professional acting debut, my first trip to Europe (in the summer of 1961, when the company represented the United States in the Theatre of Nations Festival in Paris, and won the Grand Prix), and it was here where I met my future wife, Janet Templeton. It was at the Living Theatre that I made personal contact with Dorothy Day's Catholic Worker Movement, which remains to this day a powerful source of grace in my life. And it was here that my talent was realized and flourished, and my career began in earnest. It was also here that I was exposed to nonviolence as a practical way of life.

Julian Beck was thirty-six when I met him, and although he was six feet, two inches tall, he never weighed more than 150 pounds in his adult life. This, coupled with his early loss of hair and unusually pale complexion, gave him a much older and extremely frail appearance despite his great energy.

One night as I was sweeping the stairway between floors at the theater, a very large and unruly character appeared, demanding to see one of the actors who was on stage at the time. Julian was summoned, and he politely pleaded with the man to leave a message for the actor and depart, since he was causing such a disturbance. But the man refused and became even more unruly, cursing Julian and making violent threats. Julian continued in a firm but compassionate manner to dissuade him when suddenly this fellow reared back and slapped

Julian across the face with a blow that sent him flying backward down the stairs and into my arms. I was terrified, knowing full well that this madman could destroy both of us with ease, but before I could respond, Julian righted himself, took a deep breath, and then very calmly walked back up to the man and again in the same compassionate manner asked him to leave.

The man was so completely disarmed and shamed that he simply looked away and muttered some unintelligible curse as he brushed past us, going back down the stairs and out the door. In that instant the personal cost of nonviolence was made as clear to me as the blood red imprint of the man's hand on the side of Julian's face. Each time I face arrest during nonviolent civil disobedience actions for peace and social justice, I remember how extraordinary and ironic that such a frail man could teach such a powerful and lifelong lesson. I was nineteen years old then, and I had never seen such an astonishing nonviolent response to such an aggressive act. And I had been raised a Catholic in the faith of the nonviolent Jesus.

One day in 1963 I gave a very energetic audition for a New York Shakespeare Festival public high school touring company production of *Macbeth*. The director was sufficiently impressed to offer me a small role for very little money, which I politely and promptly rejected, since I was married with a growing family to support. In retrospect, I should have eagerly accepted the role despite the hardship it promised, since it would have united me with theater icon and future mentor Joseph Papp much earlier. This handsome, complex, delightfully pugnacious, disarmingly humorous, deeply compassionate, enviably courageous, self-educated, Brooklyn-born Shakespearean scholar was arguably the single most influential force on the American theater in the twentieth century. Like everyone who loved him, I called him Joe, and he was the only man, other than my father, who called me Ramon, my real name.

I worked with Joe many times over the years in productions of *Antony and Cleopatra, Hamlet,* and *Julius Caesar.* But the one I chiefly loved was *Romeo and Juliet* in which Joe directed and I played Romeo in the summer of 1968 for a Central Park production. A few days into rehearsal we were working on the famous so-called Queen Mab scene, where Mercutio first appears with dazzling speeches and overwhelming energy. It suddenly occurred to me that I was playing the wrong part. I should have been playing Mercutio, and not Romeo. I concocted a scenario that I presented to Joe after rehearsal in the hope that he would see the wisdom of my decision and make the switch.

Ever careful not to offend the great Shakespearean maestro for a casting error, and quick to express my deep gratitude for his boundless faith in trusting me with the title role, I pleaded my case for the role of Mercutio with passion. "Let's face it, Joe," I said. "I am not a lovesick and dull Romeo type, rather an energetic and heroic Mercutio type." On and on I went, from the time it took us to walk from the rehearsal hall up three flights of stairs and across the lobby to his office. Along the way Joe listened patiently, never interrupting my diatribe as he unwrapped and prepared a fresh cigar.

As I concluded my argument, he looked me in the eye and without hesitation said, "Of course you could play Mercutio. It's not a real challenge for you. That's why you must play Romeo." As I absorbed the truthful shock of his remark, he lit the cigar and said, "Good night, Romeo. See you at rehearsal tomorrow."

It is not possible to overstate the measure of influence these three extraordinary men had on every aspect of my life. Nor can I account for my remarkably good fortune to have known and loved them any more than I can comprehend the immeasurable conduit of grace their lives still impart to me long after their deaths. But when I was asked to be a mentor myself, my response was a foregone conclusion, thanks to three guys called Al, Julian, and Joe and the profound effect they had on a boy named Ramon.

MICHAEL STRAHAN
YOU HAVE TO BE WILLING TO LEARN

My father was a major in the army, and in 1981 we moved to Germany. I never played organized sports in Germany, but my father always kept me active there, taking me to work out in the gym or to go fishing. He always stressed self-sufficiency and hard work. "You get out of life what you put into it," he would tell me. We would work out, and most of the time it was the last thing I wanted to do on a Sunday. I would rather have been playing with my friends. "Keep working," my dad would say. "Someday this will all pay off."

It's almost as if my dad had a crystal ball, that he knew I would play professional sports.

In the beginning of my senior year in high school, Dad wanted me to return to the United States and try to get a football scholarship to a university. I thought he was crazy. I hadn't played football since I was eight years old. My father was very encouraging and made me feel that I was a better player than I actually was. He convinced me that I was capable, so I returned to the States and moved in with my dad's brother. I started playing football for Westbury High School and eventually did get a scholarship to Texas Southern University.

I wanted to quit during my first semester. I went back to Germany for Christmas holidays and brought everything from my dorm room with me. I even took my alarm clock. When it was time for me to return to school at the end of the holiday, I told my dad that I wasn't going back. He asked what I was going to do. I said that I wanted to stay in Germany and work with him at his transport company. He had since left the army and started his own business. After a slight pause he asked again what I was going to do. He made it very clear that working at his company was not an option. So I went back to school. Back at college, I realized that it was time for me to take all these lessons of self-sufficiency and hard work and put them to use. Three years later, after my senior year, I was drafted by the New York Giants.

The biggest influence for me in football was my first professional coach, Earl Leggett. Known as the Big Man, he was a former first-round draft pick himself.

Going into the game, I really didn't know all that much about football. In Germany, I watched games on TV with my dad and read all the sports magazines. I knew enough about the game that, from the viewpoint of the defense, a quarterback sack was a good thing, and when I started playing in high school that's all I tried to do. I was big enough and fast enough to be a good player and naturally gifted enough to play football in college, but I had no technique. I had no sense of the strategy of the game. Thank God for Earl Leggett.

Coach Leggett taught me technique and showed how the repetition of drills and practice slowly became instinct, something performed almost unconsciously. He was an amazing teacher. He taught me to watch films of the other teams and to take notes critically. He showed me how to think like my opponents, how to anticipate their every move and adjust my game in the middle of the action accordingly. He explained the science of the game.

You have to be willing to learn, no matter how old you are. You have to get your ego out of the way, and being in the big leagues, you have to deal with a lot of ego. There are guys who feel that they are too big to learn or listen to anyone. As a result, everything becomes a conflict for them. It's sad. The coaches are only trying to make their team—*our* team—the best it can be, but some guys don't take it that way. To them it's all a personal insult because they aren't willing to admit that there are others who know a great deal more than they do. You go a lot further realizing that these people are here to help you and not to hurt you.

This applies to so many areas, not just football. In business, in school, in relationships, you've got to realize that you don't have the final answers, that you do need other people to help you out. And if you are open to that help, you'll be a lot happier and a lot more successful.

Three last bits of advice my father taught me: One, the best way to break a bad habit like drugs or alcohol is to never start it; two, never ask someone to give you anything—always earn it first; three, if being successful was easy, everybody would do it, so you have to work hard for success.

JOE TORRE

NEVER GIVE UP
ON YOUR DREAMS

There are two individuals who have profoundly influenced my life: my older brother Frank and my wife, Ali.

I was the youngest of five children, all of whom were big baseball fans; I grew up surrounded by the game. Frank was more of a father figure than an older brother in that he paved my way through high school. He had also been a professional baseball player, so I guess you can say that he paved the road for me in my baseball career. He let me know what to expect and how hard I needed to work. Therefore, a compliment from him was worth more than anything. He was a tough taskmaster, but an inspiration nonetheless. There is a great difference in him now as compared to a few years ago, before he had his heart transplant. Today he is traveling and active, his spirit revived and his passion for life thriving. Without his support and inspiration, there would have been a large void in my life.

Baseball was a natural interest of Frank's, as it was with me. However, I was a New York Giants fan growing up, which was a dangerous thing to be, living in Brooklyn. I was never a Yankees fan, yet I now have four World Series rings with the team.

The story goes like this: In November 1995 I was offered the manager's position with the Yankees; my daughter Andrea was born that December. Here I was at age fifty-five on the last few holes of an old golf course and another opportunity was about to open up for me. I have felt incredibly blessed, and things have been nonstop wonderful ever since.

My wife, Ali, has also been a great source of inspiration and influence on my life in telling me to never give up my dreams. When I was fired from my manager's position with the Atlanta Braves in October 1984, she stood by my side and was always there for me. I remember watching a TV show with her and the theme was "How Do You Want to Be Remembered?" Ali turned to me and asked that very question.

When I responded, "Someone who never accomplished what he wanted," she saw how down I was and kept my spirits up for the five or six years that I went into broadcasting.

During that time, I realized that when you are behind the mike for a while, you start to lose your competitive nature and forget how it feels to win; you lose the competitive nature of winning and losing. At that point in my career, and with that realization, having not won a World Series left me empty. Then, in 1990, I received a call from Dal Maxvill, a former teammate of mine and general manager of the St. Louis Cardinals. He offered me the position of manager and I stayed there until 1995, when I was fired early on in the season. Then Arthur Richman, a member of the Yankees organization who had been around baseball for nearly sixty years, called in November of that year and asked if I was interested in managing the Yankees. This was a welcome opportunity, albeit a surprising offer.

After the 1996 season, people were looking back and saying how much of that season was about my personal story, the personal battles in my life: My brother Rocco died in June and then Frank needed a heart transplant. The season was painted as a battle and then triumph for me. I was asked more than once: "Now that you've accomplished what you have wanted for so long, are you going to retire?"

"No," I said. "Why desert the coaches and players?"

Nineteen ninety-six was a magical year, and I credit Ali with keeping my desire for baseball alive, my feet on the ground, and enabling me to return to coaching after broadcasting.

She was there for me again in 1997, when, after the first month of the season in early May, I wasn't having fun anymore. People only seemed occupied with getting another World Series win and asking me if that was all I wanted to accomplish, and now that I had that, what was I going to do. This preoccupation bothered me to the point that it caused me not to be happy and not to have fun. Ali pointed this out and said, "I don't know you anymore."

When I told her what was bothering me, she said, "What do you care what people think?"

She was right. From that moment on, I have never looked back. And life has been fantastic.

I also thank George Steinbrenner for allowing me that opportunity to win. He did this by signing good players and allowing me to reap the benefits of coaching them. You cannot win the Kentucky Derby with a quarter horse; you need the caliber of a thoroughbred.

STANLEY TUCCI

GO BEYOND
WHAT IS COMFORTABLE

In my sophomore year of high school I auditioned for Gilbert Freeman, the drama and chorus teacher, with a comic skit that I had written. It was during the audition that I realized how at ease I felt onstage. Gil recognized this, and for the next three years instructed and encouraged me in the performing arts.

He always encouraged his students to take advantage of the city and its cultural life. Though not a professional actor or director himself, he more than understood the basic principles of acting and was very articulate in communicating them to high school students—not an easy task. To this day, I am thankful for his encouragement, and I make use of the simple but invaluable tools he gave me.

After high school I went to college at SUNY Purchase, an arts conservatory where I was fortunate enough to have George Morrison as my mentor. It was a very challenging and enormously freeing four years. But of all the myriad brilliant things George taught us, there is a single phrase or tenet that echoes every day in my mind: "Go beyond what's comfortable." There are no more important words for any artist.

Of all the artists and teachers who have influenced me along the way, I would say that my father would rank first and foremost. He is both an artist and a teacher, having been the head of the art department at Horace Greeley High School in Chappaqua, New York. From the time I was four or five years old, I would accompany him to his summer school classes and the Saturday classes he taught throughout the year. As a teacher he had humor and patience, adapting himself easily to each student's needs, personality, and ability. Most important, he taught without judgment, believing that grades should not even be given in art. Effort was the only thing that he knew could be judged. It was for these reasons that I grew up not being afraid of my creative impulses, but following them.

This was not the norm for a boy growing up in a small town like Katonah, New York. In suburban America, boys are athletes and little more is expected of them other than good grades. But because both my parents encouraged creativity as well as athleticism and my dad had devoted his life to teaching art—and to the idea that creative expression and art in general was a necessity and not a luxury—I could not help but choose a life in the arts. It is a life that I am very proud of and hope that through my work I can instill the same feelings in others that he invoked in me.

To this day whenever I encounter my father's students, whether they are artists or not, they all remember him as one of the best teachers they ever had. I can only agree with them.

MEREDITH VIEIRA

CONFIDENCE HAS TO COME
FROM WITHIN

Early in my career, I was working as a reporter in Providence, Rhode Island, and I was abruptly fired on a Friday. My boss told me he didn't think I had what it takes to do the job. I went home to my parents' house in Rumford crying. When I told my dad, he asked, "Well, do you think you have what it takes?" I said, "Yes, I think I do." The advice he gave me next proved to be a critical lesson.

"What this person says is irrelevant then," he advised. "You're going to have people throughout your life tell you you're not good enough, or can't do this or that, or you don't have what it takes. Confidence has to come from within, and you'll exude more if you believe in yourself."

On Monday, I went back to work and confronted the man who had fired me. He hired me back right on the spot. We all have a talent, but without faith in yourself it's impossible to find success.

When I started at CBS News in the early 1980s, I was working happily in the northeast bureau in New York City. Without warning, however, they transferred me to Chicago. It was during a very tough time in the economy. Farmers were suffering, the auto industry was in trouble, and crime was on the rise. As a result, I was always on the air. It was a great blessing for a young, green reporter to have that much exposure, but on the downside, I wasn't feeling a lot of support. Luckily for me, there was one person willing to take me under his wing.

Howard Stringer, well known today as the legendary broadcast journalist, producer, and executive of Sony Corporation, was the executive producer of *CBS Evening News* when I was starting out. He was the one who helped me polish my writing and reporting skills. He was my biggest fan from the very beginning.

He would look at my scripts and critique them, but never in a demoralizing way. That wasn't his MO. He would ask me, "Did you consider this?" or "Why did you make this decision?" He knew that there was a way to do it better, but somehow he always made me feel like I'd come up with the answer myself. I would leave the meeting with him complimenting my brilliance, even though he was the one who led me to the answer.

Like a true mentor, he didn't give me my voice, but he helped define it, nurture it, and develop it. He taught me to listen—really listen and let the story come to you. Every reporter has to learn to pay attention to the people telling the stories, and Howard was the one who instilled that skill in me.

When the *Today* show suggested a segment on mentors and inspirations, I immediately stepped up to do a story on Howard. He is someone I will always treasure for helping to shape my career.

When I mentor the new generation of young journalists, I try to pass on the nurturing, confidence, and support from my parents and Howard. With Howard in mind, I tell them to listen. It's one thing to hear; but another thing to listen. There are distinct differences. And whether you're covering a pie sale in Iowa or reporting from a war zone, the values you bring to a story should be the same.

ELI WALLACH

MAKE VOYAGES

There were two people who served as mentors to me as a young actor. The first was Sanford Meisner, a great acting teacher at the Neighborhood Playhouse School of the Theatre. The other was Martha Graham, the brilliant teacher of dance technique and the Graham method at the Playhouse.

Ms. Graham taught me that movement is a great tool—I use her teaching in every character I create on stage. Mr. Meisner also helped me by making me curious about the arts. "Read, read," he'd say. "Go to museums. Let the music enter your soul."

Both mentors stiffened my spine, told me I was unique. They said I should make voyages, attempt them—there's nothing else.

The impact of having older role models outside of my family was tremendous. Both pried open the doors of my mind. They were pioneers in their field and great teachers, and they told me what I needed to hear: Don't be disheartened, stay with your choice of career, and have the grit and courage to work, work, work.

For me as an actor, the turning point was my decision to stay with the theater. Television and film were temptations, but both Mr. Meisner and Ms. Graham taught me that as an artist I had to be tied to the live theater. Their lessons have stayed with me throughout my career.

ALICE WATERS
ARTFULLY, SIMPLY,
AND WITH GRACE

I first met Lulu Peyraud nearly forty years ago, on a visit to the South of France to see the winery, Domaine Tempier, that she runs with her husband. I remember how it felt to enter the tree-lined walkway leading to the house for the first time: It seemed timeless, near-magical. Everything about Lulu—her infectious laughter, her celebration of life at the table, her deep love for the Provençal countryside—was like something out of the movies. And yet it was wholly authentic: Though she knew nothing about me (and I had only a shaky grasp of French), she embraced me as if I were a dear member of her family, sitting me down at her husband Lucien's right hand, just across from her at the lunch table. It was a big meal, with cousins and children gathered around; as we ate, Lucien would pass me the very best morsels of food. When I haltingly tried to express my gratitude in French, Lulu leaned in, smiled, and whispered, "Don't worry. I understand everything."

Through the years, I have never felt more understood than when I have been with the Peyrauds. Everyone who came to Domaine Tempier was treated with the same warmth and generosity; each guest was welcomed as if he or she were a much-loved child home for a visit. Whether we were sampling little sandwiches of sea urchin on buttered bread, or eating a fragrant bouillabaisse just as a mistral began to blow against the windows, or drinking a bracingly cold glass of rosé under their grape arbor on a scorching summer day, I always had the same sweet feeling of being at home. Lulu knew how to take care of people—effortlessly and with great joy.

In the kitchen, Lulu's inimitable presence seems to me the definition of the French expression la cuisine de bonne femme. She cooks with remarkable ease, almost unconsciously, sautéing wild mushrooms with herbs and garlic while chatting away with her guests over a welcoming glass of wine. She knows exactly what to do without ever overdoing it, and her food is often robust, always delicious, and always right for the season and the moment. And she is always present at the table, whether she's preparing for a party of thirty or a party of three.

When she is choosing ingredients, Lulu searches for flavor and freshness above all else. She walks to the fish market just as the boats are coming in and waits while the fishermen unload their catch under the canopy of plane trees, watching to see which wriggling fish looks best. The herbs she uses come from the garden behind the house or grow wild on the hillsides. Figs are gathered from her son's house down the road, and squash blossoms might come from the neighbor's little farm stand. For Lulu, food must be alive, real—there is no other way.

At ninety-one, she is as indefatigable as ever. She listens to all the news reports and brings me up to speed, carries in wood to light a fire in the hearth every morning, shells peas and fava beans as she has done for decades, and visits with her children and grandchildren at the long lunch table on the terrace under the fig arbor. Her example over the years has profoundly shaped my own life. Both at Chez Panisse and at home, I try to remain connected to the earth, going first to the garden and the fields for inspiration, and letting the food speak for itself. And of course, I gather friends and family together around the table whenever I can. I am trying to live the way Lulu lives, how she has always lived: artfully, simply, and with grace.

JAMIE WYETH

COLLECTOR OF MEMORIES
AND LESSONS

Lincoln Kirstein was interested in my development as an artist and took it upon himself to help educate me. Since he was an art enthusiast and collector, he knew my father's works and was instrumental in buying *Christina's World* for the Museum of Modern Art. When I moved to New York at sixteen, he immersed me in learning. He taught me art history firsthand, taking me through all the museums and galleries in New York. He taught me architecture, business, history—he was an amazing trove of knowledge. Our friendship grew over the years until his death in 1996.

I remember walking with him through the medieval antiquities collection at the Metropolitan Museum of Art, pointing to a helmet and saying it reminded me of something from an Eisenstein film. He nodded his head and said that he admired the Russian filmmaker. A week later, I was visiting him at his house and relating the story of the medieval collection to a friend of his when Lincoln said that he had some "things" of Eisenstein's that might be of interest to me. These "things" turned out to be volumes of drawings and sketches by the filmmaker for his unfinished epic *Que Viva Mexico!* There were pages and pages of Eisenstein's storyboards for the film and sketches of planned film shots. Lincoln had received Eisenstein's sketchbooks as a token from the director for his substantial investment in the film. He had never mentioned this to me before. He was always very quiet about his "things." He didn't like his name attached to anything and preferred to stay out of the spotlight.

Lincoln was a remarkable philanthropist. He was responsible for the founding of the New York City Ballet and, along with the Rockefellers, was instrumental in the founding of the Museum of Modern Art. He was also a founder of Lincoln Center and brought the famed Russian choreographer George Balanchine to the City Ballet.

He wore so many hats. He was a literary editor, an author, a painter, and a poet. But he had no ambition for a career as an artist. He had made up his mind at a very young age to give his life to philanthropy.

You had to self-educate yourself with Lincoln. He never said this is what you need to know; rather, he hinted at it and you had to find out about his hints. He made you make the discovery yourself.

I remember that I was fascinated with the dancer Rudolf Nureyev. I wanted to paint him but found Lincoln much against it. He said that Nureyev was a star—a grandstander who was not a company dancer—and being a "company dancer" was very much a part of Kirstein and Balanchine's vision for the New York City Ballet. Eventually I did paint Nureyev and exhibited this series. Lincoln saw the exhibit before it opened but did not comment on it. Later I learned that he had purchased one of the paintings.

Lincoln was a lone figure who didn't go to parties, premieres, or show openings. As he put it, he "wasn't housebroken." He always dressed in his own sort of uniform: a black suit, white shirt, and black tie. He was a big man with an even larger presence. When I first moved to New York, he promised that he would sit for a portrait for me. We scheduled a time for the drawing session and when I arrived at his door, I found him rushing out. "I've got no time right now; I have to go to this march in Mississippi." Naturally, Lincoln was involved in the planning of the historic Selma civil rights march. He had simply forgotten to tell me about it and we had to reschedule.

Lincoln Kirstein was a mentor for many people. There's a stereotype of the kind and gentle teacher, but typical of Lincoln, he was the opposite of what was accepted as the norm. He was not an easy man. He was very tough and extremely hard on me. But that was his way.

His influence on the arts in America has yet to be fully appreciated or understood. By arts, I'm not talking about specific disciplines such as dance or painting but the very concept of American art, as a whole, for the average person to be exposed to. Years from now, I think, he will be seen as a seminal figure for our times, not only for his monumental presence in American art but also as a social activist and engineer.

FAREED ZAKARIA
VISUALIZE THE POSSIBILITIES

*What lies behind the bumper sticker slogan is an incredibly
complex historical phenomenon. You really need to be
using your mind to analyze rather than just mouthing off.*

I grew up in India and was somewhat isolated from the rest of the
world. There were two great men who came into my life and provided enormous inspiration and helped me break through that isola-
tion and visualize the possibilities of a broader world.

My mother's boss, Khushwant Singh, one of India's great journalists and a celebrated novelist, just loved the English language. He would
recite poetry to me beginning when I was a young boy and ask me to
recite it back. He was trying to get me to memorize it, not in a strident
teaching style, but like a game that instilled a great love for words.
"Let's see how much of this you can remember?"

He really believed in broadening the human being. He taught me
to play tennis and to swim. He was a great naturalist and in long
walks into the hills would identify every plant and every bird based
on their calls. I can't remember the specifics anymore, but he gave
me the first inclination that what you do for a living, and what you
love, can become the same thing.

Girilal Jain was another leading Indian journalist who helped
expand my horizons personally and intellectually. He was an ardent

believer in social science and the power of analyzing complex phenomena. What I remember clearly is long conversations in which he would discuss an issue, break it down, and tap the power of history to help make it comprehensible and relevant.

"Do you really understand?" he asked me after I made a completely off-the-cuff and politically correct comment on the Vietnam War. He then proceeded to give me an in-depth history lesson on the country from the 1950s onward. It was one of those moments when it suddenly clicked. What lies behind the bumper sticker slogan is an incredibly complex historical phenomenon. You really need to be using your mind to analyze rather than just mouthing off.

As I try to bring the vigor of political science, the depth of history, and the power of the English language to my writing, I think of my two mentors, eight thousand miles away.

LEARN MORE ABOUT MENTORING USA

CHANGE A LIFE.
BECOME A MENTOR.

For the last two decades, Mentoring USA's mission has been to create positive mentor relationships for youth ages seven to twenty-one through a structured, site-based model. Mentoring USA encourages vulnerable youth to stay in school with the support of one-to-one consistent relationships. Mentors, along with the help of Mentoring USA's professional staff, work to ensure a productive lifestyle and a hopeful outlook for the child. The comprehensive mentoring program trains mentors to guide their mentees in building strong self-esteem, developing a healthy lifestyle, gaining respect for self and others, understanding diversity, building financial literacy, and making positive life choices.

Our annual accountability study has confirmed, time and again, the success of our program through our mentees' high rates of high school completion and progression to college.

What Mentors Say about Mentoring USA

"Mentoring at 18th Avenue School in Newark has been a highlight over the past six months, and I can't wait for school to be back in session. Watching my shy mentee go from barely making eye contact during week one to dispensing hugs, together with his ability to add and subtract fractions (yippee!), has been a thrill for me—one that I won't forget. In just a short time, I know I made a difference in a child's life—he certainly made one in mine."

—Bari J. Mattes, Senior Advisor to Mayor Cory Booker
18th Avenue School Mentor, Newark, NJ

"I decided to become a mentor so that I can provide compassionate support to a young person. This experience has surpassed my expectations. I have formed a positive relationship with my mentee, and I look forward to spending time with her during the sessions. Our sessions are filled with interesting conversations, laughter, and teaching moments. My mentee is an outspoken, energetic, well-rounded, intelligent teenager who isn't afraid to speak her mind. Our interactions allow me to think about life and what it means to be a teenager growing up in New York City. As a teenager, I didn't have formal mentors, but there were adults in my life that influenced me and encouraged me to set and achieve goals. I am grateful that I am able to be a part of my mentee's life, and I am thankful that she is a part of mine."

—Danielle Fairbairn
Mentor at Chelsea Elliott "I Have a Dream" Program, New York City

What Mentees Say about Mentoring USA

"This guy saved my life. I was heading in the wrong direction, and now I'm finishing high school."

—Mentee, Harlem Dowling Foster Care Agency

"Mentoring means for me a new experience to grow and learn with somebody who I consider a friend."

—Mentee, HELP USA, Robert F. Kennedy Apartments

"My mentor is like a big sister to me and I can always open up to her."

—Mentee, HELP USA, Robert F. Kennedy Apartments

To learn how you can become a mentor and support Mentoring USA, please call (212) 400-8294 or visit www.mentoringusa.org.

CONTRIBUTORS

Alan Alda has acted in, written, and directed many feature films in addition to the eleven years he spent on M*A*S*H. He has played vital parts in films from Woody Allen's *Crimes and Misdemeanors* to Martin Scorsese's *The Aviator*, for which he received an Academy Award nomination in 2005. He has written two best-selling books, *Never Have Your Dog Stuffed* and *Things I Overheard While Talking to Myself*. With his wife, Arlene, whom he writes about in his essay, he has been actively involved in charitable work for women and children.

Christiane Amanpour is the anchor of ABC's Sunday-morning political affairs program, *This Week with Christiane Amanpour*. On CNN, she was most recently the network's chief international correspondent and anchor of *Amanpour*, a daily half-hour interview program. She has reported on and from the world's major hot spots, including Iraq, Afghanistan, Iran, Pakistan, Somalia, Israel, the Palestinian territories, Rwanda, the Balkans, and the United States during Hurricane Katrina. Amanpour has received every major broadcast award, including an inaugural Television Academy Award, nine News and Documentary Emmys, four George Foster Peabody Awards, two George Polk Awards, three duPont-Columbia Awards, the Courage in Journalism Award, an Edward R. Murrow Award, and nine honorary degrees. In 2010 she was inducted into the American Academy of Arts and Sciences.

Dave Annable, quickly becoming one of Hollywood's most sought-after actors, can currently be seen in the ABC series *Brothers and*

Sisters. His film credits include the recent comedy *You May Not Kiss the Bride* and the 2004 hit *Little Black Book*. Annable attended college at SUNY Plattsburgh and studied acting at the famed Neighborhood Playhouse in New York City with Richard Pinter. Philanthropically, Annable has been a supporter and friend of Project ALS for many years and recently became an ambassador for the Christopher and Dana Reeve Foundation.

Edward Asner is best known for his comedic and dramatic crossover as the gruff but soft-hearted journalist Lou Grant in *The Mary Tyler Moore Show* and continued in the newspaper-set drama *Lou Grant,* which earned him five Emmys and three Golden Globe Awards. Asner received two more Emmy and Golden Globe Awards for the miniseries *Rich Man, Poor Man* and *Roots*. As well, Asner has been the recipient of seven Emmy Awards and sixteen nominations and five Golden Globe Awards.

Alec Baldwin, a graduate of New York University, has appeared in over forty films, including *Beetlejuice, Working Girl, Miami Blues, The Hunt for Red October, Glengarry Glen Ross, State and Main, The Cooler, The Aviator, The Departed,* and *It's Complicated,* among many others. On television, Baldwin currently stars with Tina Fey on NBC's *30 Rock*. Baldwin has received four SAG Awards, three Golden Globes, the Television Critics Award, and two Emmy Awards. Baldwin's book, *A Promise to Ourselves* (St. Martin's Press) was published in paperback in the fall of 2009.

William Baldwin has distinguished himself as an actor, producer, and writer who continues to showcase his multitude of talents in the world of film, television, and music. Most recently Baldwin returned to primetime TV to join the cast of *Parenthood*. He has also had recurring roles on *Gossip Girl* and *Dirty Sexy Money* and has been in more than twenty-five movies. Baldwin lives in Santa Barbara, California, with his wife, Chynna Phillips, and three children Jameson (age ten), Vance (age eight), and Brooke (age five).

Maria Bartiromo is anchor of CNBC's *Closing Bell with Maria Bartiromo* and anchor and managing editor of the nationally syndicated *Wall Street Journal Report with Maria Bartiromo*, which was recently rated the most-watched financial news program in America. In 1995, Bartiromo became the first journalist to report live from the floor of the New York Stock Exchange on a daily basis. Bartiromo is the author of several books, including *The Weekend That Changed Wall Street* and *The 10 Laws of Enduring Success,* both published in 2010.

Joy Behar is an Emmy Award–winning host of HLN's *The Joy Behar Show* and is an acclaimed star of the stage, small screen, and silver screen. Her previous television credits have included roles and guest appearances on networks including CNN, HLN, HBO, ABC, NBC, Comedy Central, and Bravo. For three years, Behar hosted her own WABC radio show. Behar, along with her cohosts on ABC's *The View,* has received twelve consecutive Daytime Emmy Award nominations for Outstanding Talk Show Host.

Harry Belafonte is as well-known for his social activism and pursuit of social justice as he is for his award-winning acting and musical talent. His album *Calypso* made him the first artist in history to sell more than one million LPs. He won a Tony Award for his Broadway debut in *John Murray Anderson's Almanac* and an Emmy for *An Evening with Belafonte,* in which he was also the first black producer in television. He was also awarded the National Medal for the Arts by President Clinton. He has been equally recognized in the social justice arena, with honors such as the Albert Einstein Award from Yeshiva University, the Martin Luther King Jr. Peace Prize, and the Nelson Mandela Courage Award. He has served as a UNICEF Goodwill Ambassador and is a recipient of the prestigious Kennedy Center Honors for excellence in the performing arts.

Tony Bennett is an artist who moves the hearts and touches the souls of audiences. He's not just the singer's singer but also an international treasure honored by the United Nations with its Citizen of the World award, which aptly describes the scope of his accomplishments. With worldwide record sales in the millions and dozens of platinum and gold albums to his credit, Bennett has received fifteen Grammy Awards, including the prestigious Grammy Lifetime Achievement Award. Tony Bennett became a Kennedy Center Honoree in 2005 and was named an NEA Jazz Master in January 2006 and was also named the recipient of *Billboard* magazine's elite Century Award, in honor of his outstanding contributions to music.

Michael R. Bloomberg is the one hundred eighth mayor of the city of New York. He is also the founder of the global media company Bloomberg LP and one of the world's most generous philanthropists.

Andrea Bocelli, born in Lajatico, Italy, in 1958, has scaled the heights of both popular and classical music. He has performed to packed houses in celebrated venues all over the world, including the Colosseum in Rome and the Metropolitan Opera House in New York City. He has shared the stage with such stars as Celine Dion and Placido Domingo. His albums have sold more than 70 million copies, making him the best-selling classical solo artist of all time; he's also featured in the *Guinness Book of World Records* for simultaneously holding the top three positions on the American classical music sales charts. In 2010 he was given a star on the Hollywood Walk of Fame.

Cory Booker is the mayor of Newark, New Jersey. He took the oath of office as mayor of New Jersey's largest city on July 1, 2006, and was reelected to a second term on May 11, 2010. Mayor Booker is a member of numerous boards and advisory committees, including Democrats for Education Reform, Columbia University Teachers' College Board of Trustees, and the Black Alliance for Educational Options. Mayor Booker received his BA and MA from Stanford University and a BA in modern history from Oxford University as a Rhodes Scholar, and completed his law degree at Yale University.

Senator William W. Bradley, age sixty-seven, is a managing director of Allen & Company LLC. From 2001 to 2004, he acted as chief outside advisor to McKinsey & Company's nonprofit practice. Senator Bradley served in the US Senate from 1979 to 1997 representing the state of New Jersey. In 2000, he was a candidate for the Democratic nomination for President of the United States. Prior to serving in the Senate, he was an Olympic gold medalist in 1964 and a professional basketball player with the New York Knicks from 1967 to 1977, during which time they won two NBA championships. In 1982, he was elected to the Basketball Hall of Fame. Senator Bradley holds a BA in American history from Princeton University and a master's degree from Oxford University, where he was a Rhodes Scholar. He has authored six books on American politics, culture, and economy, including his latest book, *The New American Story.*

James S. Brady and his wife, Sarah, have been tireless champions of sensible gun laws. Brady achieved a lifelong career goal when President Ronald Reagan appointed him assistant to the president and White House press secretary in January of 1981. His service, however, was cut short on March 30, 1981, when a mentally deranged young man, John Hinckley, attempted to assassinate the president and shot both President Reagan, Brady, and two law enforcement officers. Brady suffered a serious head wound that left him partially paralyzed for life. Since leaving the White House, he has spent countless hours lobbying for commonsense gun laws. On November 30, 1993, President Bill Clinton signed the Brady Handgun Violence Protection Act, also known as the Brady Bill, into law. In 1996, Brady received the Presidential Medal of Freedom, the highest civilian award in the United States.

Helen Gurley Brown was born in Green Forest, Arkansas. In 1962, she published *Sex and the Single Girl,* which became a bestseller. The book was published in twenty-eight countries and translated into sixteen languages. Her other books include *Sex and the Office,* also a bestseller, and *The Outrageous Opinions of Helen Gurley Brown.* In 1965, Brown became editor in chief of *Cosmopolitan* magazine, and the rest is publishing history. Today there are thirty-six international editions of the magazine; since 1997, Brown serves as editor in chief of all foreign-language versions. Brown was inducted into the Publisher's Hall of Fame in 1988. She is, in her words, "a health nut, a feminist, an irredeemable but contented workaholic, and passionately interested in the relationship between men and women."

Richard Chai, a New York native, began his career in fashion at an early age with a prestigious internship at Geoffrey Beene as an undergraduate at Parsons School of Design. He has worked as an assistant designer at Armani Exchange and as a designer at Donna Karan for the DKNY and D collections. From 1998 to 2001, Chai was the design director for the Marc Jacobs' men's and women's collections and the launch of the Marc by Marc Jacobs men's line. In September 2001, Chai was appointed creative design director of all TSE brands, marking the first time in the company's history that a single person oversaw all brands. Richard Chai established his own company in 2004.

Hillary Rodham Clinton was sworn in as the sixty-seventh Secretary of State of the United States on January 21, 2009. Secretary Clinton joined the State Department after nearly four decades in public service as an advocate, attorney, First Lady, and senator. Secretary Clinton is the author of best-selling books, including her memoir, *Living History,* and her groundbreaking book on children, *It Takes a Village.*

William Jefferson Clinton was the first Democratic president in six decades to be elected twice—first in 1992 and then in 1996. Under his leadership, the country enjoyed the strongest economy in a generation and the longest economic expansion in US history. After leaving the White House, President Clinton established the William J. Clinton Foundation with the mission to strengthen the capacity of people in the United States and throughout the world to meet the challenges of global interdependence.

Kenneth Cole has been on the front line of fashion trends and AIDS awareness throughout his career. As a renowned American designer and humanitarian, Cole believes: "It is great to be known for your shoes. It is even better to be recognized for your soul." A business that began over twenty-five years ago out of the back of a forty-foot trailer, Kenneth Cole Productions has risen to the top of American fashion.

Cindy Crawford is known to the world as one of the original supermodels who defined that pivotal moment when fashion models became stars in their own right. Crawford's career has spanned over two decades and resulted in an exceedingly successful and trusted brand representing beauty, fashion, fitness, and home.

Walter Cronkite was a pioneer broadcast journalist and a longtime champion of journalism values who began his distinguished career as a wire service reporter. Cronkite was the chief correspondent covering the Nuremberg trials and reported on the pivotal stories of the 1960s and 1970s—the assassination of John F. Kennedy, the battles over civil rights, the Vietnam War, the Apollo moon landings, and the Watergate scandal. Cronkite was the recipient of a Peabody Award, the William Allen White Award for Journalistic Merit, an Emmy Award from the Academy of Television Arts and Sciences, the George Polk Award, and a Gold Medal Award from the International Radio and Television Society. Cronkite died in 2009.

Andrew M. Cuomo was elected the fifty-sixth Governor of New York State on November 2, 2010. Throughout his life, Cuomo has been a forceful voice for change in New York. His leadership as Attorney General has led to numerous industry-wide investigations—exposing corrupt practices within both Albany and the private sector. His lifelong commitment to hard work, public service, and the people he serves has led to Cuomo's recognition as a true innovator and a principled and determined leader.

Christopher Cuomo is the co-anchor of *20/20*, the Emmy Award–winning ABC newsmagazine, and the chief law and justice correspondent for ABC News, covering legal and breaking news for the entire network. Previously, Cuomo was the news anchor for *Good Morning America* beginning in 2006, and he co-anchored the newsmagazine

Primetime, which he joined in 2004. Cuomo's reporting and investigations have been recognized with more than a dozen journalism awards, including a Loeb Award for business reporting, multiple Emmy nominations, and a News Emmy Award.

Mario M. Cuomo was elected New York State's fifty-fourth Governor in 1982 and won reelection in both 1986 and 1990, setting records for popularity in both contests. He was the longest serving Democratic governor in the modern history of New York State and won the two largest electoral victories ever. He is the author and editor of several books, most recently *Why Lincoln Matters, Today More Than Ever.*

Ossie Davis was born Raiford Chatman Davis in Cogdell, Georgia. His acting career, which spanned seven decades, began in 1939 with the Rose McClendon Players in Harlem. He made his film debut in 1950 in the Sidney Poitier film *No Way Out.* In addition to acting, Davis was one of the notable African American directors of his generation. In 1948, Davis married actress Ruby Dee. Davis and Dee were recipients of the Kennedy Center Honors in 2004. They were also named to the NAACP Image Awards Hall of Fame in 1989.

Dr. Djibril Diallo is a senior advisor to the executive director of UNAIDS and helps advance the priority of universal access to HIV/AIDS prevention, treatment, care, and support. His work for peace and sustainable development has been recognized by numerous national and international organizations.

Fran Drescher is a two-time Emmy and Golden Globe nominee for her portrayal as the lovable Miss Fine on the CBS hit series *The Nanny,* a show she also created, wrote, directed, and executive produced. More recently, she starred in the WB series *Living with Fran* and recently guest-starred on the HBO hit series *Entourage.* Both of her books, *Enter Whining* and *Cancer Schmancer* were *New York Times* bestsellers. A uterine cancer survivor, Drescher celebrated nine years of wellness on June 21, 2009. Today she is the president of the Cancer Schmancer Movement, a nonprofit organization.

Marian Wright Edelman, founder and president of the Children's Defense Fund, has been an advocate for disadvantaged Americans for her entire professional life. A graduate of Spelman College and Yale Law School, Edelman was the first black woman admitted to the Mississippi Bar and also directed the NAACP Legal Defense and Educational Fund office in Jackson, Mississippi. She has received many awards, including the Albert Schweitzer Humanitarian Prize, the Heinz Award, a MacArthur Foundation Prize Fellowship, the Presidential Medal of Freedom—the nation's highest civilian award—and the Robert F. Kennedy Lifetime Achievement Award for her writings, which include *Families in Peril; The Measure of Our Success; Lanterns; I'm Your Child, God; I Can Make a Difference;* and *The Sea Is So Wide and My Boat Is So Small.*

Nora Ephron is a journalist, novelist, playwright, screenwriter, and director. Her credits include *Heartburn, When Harry Met Sally, Sleepless in Seattle, You've Got Mail,* and the recent *Julie & Julia.* She received three Oscar nominations for screenwriting. Her books include *Crazy Salad; Scribble, Scribble; Heartburn; I Feel Bad About My Neck,* a number one bestseller; and *I Remember Nothing.* Her play *Love, Loss, and What I Wore,* written with her sister Delia Ephron, is currently running Off-Broadway at the Westside Theatre in New York and at the Geffen Theater in Los Angeles.

Gloria Estefan exploded onto the pop scene in 1985 as the dynamic front woman of the groundbreaking Miami Sound Machine. An astonishing ninety million copies of her albums have sold worldwide, earning her the title of "the Queen of Latin Pop." As one of the most revered Hispanic female role models, Estefan has received numerous recognitions and honors. Estefan's greatest pride is her family, Nayib (age thirty) and Emily Marie (age sixteen), and her marriage of thirty-two years with her husband, Emilio Estefan.

Sarah Ferguson, Duchess of York, met Prince Andrew, the Duke of York, in 1985. The couple married the following year in Westminster Abbey and had two children, Beatrice and Eugenie. She is the author of an autobiography, some dieting guides, and several children's books. In 2011, the Oprah Winfrey Network will produce a six-part documentary series titled *Finding Sarah*, which will star the Duchess of York.

Geraldine Ferraro was the first woman nominated by a major political power as its candidate for Vice President of the United States. A teacher and then attorney, Ferraro worked in the Queens, New York, District Attorney's office, where she started the Special Victims Bureau. Ferraro ran successfully for Congress from New York City's 9th District in 1978. There, she was a women's and human rights advocate, working for passage of the Equal Rights Amendment, sponsoring the Women's Economic Equity Act ending pension discrimination against women, and seeking greater job training and opportunities for displaced homemakers.

Laurence Fishburne's work as an actor, producer, and director has garnered many impressive awards, including a Tony, a Drama Desk Award, an Outer Critics Circle Award, and an Emmy. He was nominated for an Oscar for Best Actor in 1993 for his portrayal of Ike Turner in the film *What's Love Got to Do with It*. Fishburne is as an Ambassador for UNICEF. In 2007, Harvard University honored Fishburne with an Artist of the Year Award.

Sir David Frost has not only won all the major television awards, his professional activities have been so diverse that he has been described as "a one-man conglomerate." Frost is the host and cocreator of *That Was the Week That Was*, producer of countless television programs, author of seventeen books, producer of seven films, publisher, lecturer, impresario, and the joint founder of two major network companies in the United Kingdom. His many major television awards include two Emmy Awards, the Royal Television Society Silver Medal, and the Richard Dimbleby Award in the United Kingdom, and, internationally, the Golden Rose of Montreux.

Whoopi Goldberg is one of a very elite group of artists who have won the Grammy, Academy, Golden Globe, Emmy, and Tony awards for her roles in films such as *Ghost, The Color Purple,* and AMC's *Beyond Tara,* as well as for her work as a producer of Broadway's *Thoroughly Modern Millie* and as host of ABC's *The View.* She is equally well-known for her humanitarian efforts on behalf of children, the homeless, human rights, education, substance abuse, and the battle against AIDS, as well as many other causes and charities. Among her many charitable activities, Goldberg is a Goodwill Ambassador to the United Nations.

Tipper Gore is an author, advocate, photographer, and the former Second Lady of the United States. Throughout her many years of public service, she has shared her warmth, charm, and infectious energy with communities and organizations around the globe, and used her unique position and perspective to advocate on behalf of families, women, and children on issues of mental health, homelessness, and violence in the media. She's been both an advisor on the highest policy levels, as well as a hands-on service provider to those in need in her community.

Charles Grodin was born Charles Grodinsky on April 21, 1935, in Pittsburgh, Pennsylvania. Grodin studied acting with Lee Strasberg and Uta Hagen. He played small but memorable roles throughout the late 1960s, receiving his big break in 1972 when he landed the lead in *The Heartbreak Kid.* Throughout the 1980s, Grodin turned in a number of acclaimed supporting roles in such films as *The Woman in Red* (1984), *The Couch Trip* (1987) and *The Lonely Guy* (1984). Grodin published his autobiography, *It Would Be So Nice If You Weren't Here,* in 1988.

Ray Halbritter has been the federal Representative of the Oneida Indian Nation since 1975 and CEO of its enterprises since 1990. He has led the Oneida people to an economic and cultural renaissance over the past thirty years. His accomplishments include achieving federal government recognition of the Nation's traditional form of government, creating numerous health and social programs for Nation members, constructing new housing, and establishing education and culture programs. He has a BS in business administration from Syracuse University and a JD from Harvard Law School.

Pete Hamill is a novelist, essayist, and journalist whose career has endured for more than forty years. He was born in Brooklyn in 1935, the oldest of seven children of immigrants from Belfast, Northern Ireland. In 1960, he went to work as a reporter for the *New York Post*. A long career in journalism followed. He has been a columnist for the *New York Post*, the *New York Daily News*, and *New York Newsday*, the *Village Voice*, *New York Magazine*, and *Esquire*. He has served as editor in chief of both the *Post* and the *Daily News*. He has published nine novels and two collections of short stories.

Marcia Gay Harden, an award-winning actress, has forged a remarkable body of work. From the glamorous Ava Gardner in *Sinatra* and the artist Lee Krasner in *Pollock* (for which she won the Best Supporting Actress Oscar) to the down-and-out Celeste in *Mystic River* (for which she received an Oscar nomination), Harden has created a signature style based on character transformation. Her versatility and wide range have been praised in such films as *Miller's Crossing*, *The First Wives Club*, *Meet Joe Black*, *Mona Lisa Smile*, *The Hoax*, and *Used People*. She recently garnered a Best Actress Tony Award for her starring role in the Tony Award–winning Broadway play *God of Carnage*.

Kitty Carlisle Hart wore a cloak of many professional and elegant colors. Actress, opera singer, Broadway performer, TV celebrity, game show panelist, patron of the arts, and, at age ninety-five, this vital woman continued her six-decade musical odyssey with songs and reminisces in her one-woman show, *Kitty Carlisle Hart: An American Icon*, which toured from her beloved New York to Los Angeles. She passed away of congestive heart failure in April of 2007. Carlisle Hart penned her autobiography, *Kitty*, in 1984.

Julia Butterfly Hill is an activist, writer, and poet. She is the author of the national bestseller *The Legacy of Luna* and the coauthor of *One Makes the Difference*. She brought international attention to the plight of the world's last remaining ancient forests when she climbed one hundred eighty feet into the branches of a one-thousand-year-old redwood tree and refused to come down for seven hundred thirty-eight days. In 1999, she founded the nonprofit organization Circle of Life to promote the sustainability, restoration, and preservation of life. She has since gone on to cofound the Engage Network and What's Your Tree and is a founding and ongoing advisor and donor to Women's Earth Alliance.

Anne Jackson was born Anna June Jackson in Millvale, Pennsylvania. Jackson trained at New York City's Neighborhood Playhouse and The Actor's Studio. She made her Broadway debut in 1945. Her many theater, film, and television credits include *Summer and Smoke, The Waltz of the Toreadors, The Tiger Makes Out, The Secret Life of an American Wife, The Shining, The Philco Television Playhouse, Studio One, The Untouchables, Rhoda, Law & Order,* and *ER*. Jackson has been married to actor Eli Wallach, with whom she has acted frequently, since March 5, 1948. They have three children, Peter, Katherine, and Roberta.

James Earl Jones is known for his powerful and critically acclaimed motion picture, television, and theater performances. His performance in the Alan Paton classic *Cry, The Beloved Country* promises to remain in the annals of acting studies. He is the winner of two Tony Awards. He had also received critical praise for his autobiography *James Earl Jones: Voices and Silences,* which he coauthored with Penelope Niven.

Van Jones is a globally recognized, award-winning pioneer in human rights and the clean-energy economy. Jones is a cofounder of three successful nonprofit organizations: the Ella Baker Center for Human Rights, Color of Change, and Green for All. He is the best-selling author of the definitive book on green jobs, *The Green-Collar*

Economy. He served as the green jobs advisor in the Obama White House in 2009. Jones is currently a senior fellow at the Center for American Progress and a senior policy advisor at Green for All.

Larry King is the former host of CNN's *Larry King Live*, the first worldwide phone-in television talk show and the network's highest-rated program. He celebrated his fiftieth year in broadcasting in 2007. The Emmy Award–winning King is the author of multiple books and has been dubbed "the most remarkable talk-show host on TV ever" by *TV Guide* and "master of the mike" by *Time* magazine.

Edward I. Koch was the mayor of New York City for three terms from 1978 to 1989. He saved the city of New York from bankruptcy and restored the pride of New Yorkers. Prior to being mayor, Koch served for nine years as a congressman and two years as a member of the New York City Council. He is currently a partner in the law firm of Bryan Cave LLP. Additionally, Koch is the author of numerous books, including *Mayor, Politics, His Eminence and Hizzoner, All the Best, Citizen Koch, Ed Koch on Everything, Giuliani, I'm Not Done Yet*, and most recently *Eddie, Harold's Little Brother*, a children's book that he coauthored with his sister, Pat Koch Thaler.

Dr. Mathilde Krim founded the AIDS Medical Foundation (AMF) in 1983, the first private organization concerned with fostering and supporting AIDS research. In 1985, AMF merged with another group to form the American Foundation for AIDS Research (amfAR), the preeminent national nonprofit organization devoted to mobilizing the public's generosity in support of trailblazing laboratory and clinical AIDS research, AIDS prevention, and the development of sound, AIDS-related public policies. Dr. Krim holds sixteen doctorates honoris causa and has received many other honors and distinctions. In August of 2000 she was awarded the Presidential Medal of Freedom—the highest civilian honor in the United States.

Evelyn H. Lauder, senior corporate vice president of the Esteé Lauder Companies Inc., has held many positions at the company while contributing her invaluable insights about fashion trends, consumers' changing needs, and new approaches to the development of innovative skin care, makeup, and fragrance products. She also helped create and name the Clinique brand. She is passionately committed to preventing breast cancer and finding a cure in our lifetime. In 1989, Mrs. Lauder initiated the fundraising drive that established the Evelyn H. Lauder Breast Center at Memorial Sloan-Kettering Cancer Center in New York City. Mrs. Lauder is chairman of the Breast Cancer Research Foundation (BCRF), which she founded.

Maya Lin is the world-renowned architect of the Vietnam Veterans Memorial in Washington, DC, which she designed as a twenty-one-year-old architecture student at Yale, and one of the most important public artists of this century. In 2000 Lin published her first book, *Boundaries*. Over the last decade, Maya Lin has pursued simultaneous careers as artist and architect, creating large-scale, site-specific installations and intimate studio artworks, as well as architectural works and memorials.

Sirio Maccioni, working his way on a transatlantic cruise liner, dazzled New York with his charm and acumen for hospitality. In 1974, Maccioni opened what was destined to become a New York landmark: Le Cirque, which literally translates as "the circus" in French, at the Mayfair Hotel. By 2004, Le Cirque was an established New York City institution and moved to the prestigious Bloomberg Building on East 58th Street, opening its doors in May of 2006.

Howard S. Maier is president of Maier Ventures, a marketing company with headquarters in Great Neck, New York. He is also the president of Yoga Zone LLC, a chain of yoga studios in the New York metropolitan area. Before establishing Maier Ventures, Mr. Maier was president of the Maier Group, which he sold to Time Warner in 1994. The Maier Group was a producer of nontheatrical videos and was the country's leading marketer of exercise videos, most notably the Buns of Steel series. The Maier Group ranked on INC. 500's list of the fastest-growing private companies for four successive years (1991–1994). Mr. Maier was a 1993 Entrepreneur of the Year finalist.

Mr. Maier devotes significant time to charitable organizations. He is the chairman of the Holocaust Memorial and Tolerance Center of Nassau County, a trustee of North Shore/Long Island Jewish Health System, and vice chairman of the board of directors of Gilda's Club Worldwide for cancer patients. He received a BS from the State University of New York at Buffalo in 1968 and an MBA from the Bernard M. Baruch Graduate School of Business in 1972.

Peter Max was born in Berlin in 1937, but his family moved to China when he was still very young. Max was trained at the Art Students League, Pratt Institute, and the School of Visual Arts, all in New York. From visionary pop artist of the 1960s to master of dynamic Neo-Expressionism, Peter Max and his vibrant colors have become part of the fabric of contemporary American culture.

John McCain was elected to the US Senate in 1986 and was the 2008 Republican presidential nominee. Previously, he served in the US Navy and as a US congressman for two terms. He has seven children and four grandchildren. He and his wife, Cindy, reside in Phoenix.

Midori is recognized not only for the evolution and scope of her twenty-eight-year career as one of the most dazzlingly gifted violinists and performers before the public. Named a Messenger of Peace by UN Secretary General Ban Ki-moon in 2007, she has created a new model for young artists who seek to balance the joys and demands of a performing career at the highest level with a hands-on investment in the power of music to change lives.

Ann Moore is one of the most powerful executives in the media world. As former chairman and chief executive officer of Time Inc., she oversaw the world's leading magazine company—one hundred fifteen magazines with 250 million readers worldwide. Moore has also helped spearhead several of Time Inc.'s important volunteer and philanthropic initiatives relating to education. Her numerous awards and honors include her appearance on *Fortune* magazine's list of "The 50 Most Powerful Women in American Business" for all eleven years of its existence. A native of McLean, Virginia, Moore graduated from Vanderbilt University in 1971 and received her MBA from Harvard Business School in 1978.

Josie Natori is the founder and CEO of the Natori Company, a lifestyle brand that includes lingerie collections (Josie Natori, Natori, Josie, and N Natori), the Josie Natori ready-to-wear collection, and home, fragrance, and eyewear products. Natori sits on the boards of the Asian Cultural Council, the Orchestra of St. Luke's, the Statue of Liberty-Ellis Island Foundation, Women in Need, and the Fashion and Design Council of the Philippines.

Jessye Norman's latest recording, *Roots: My Life, My Song,* was nominated for a 2010 Grammy Award. Most recently, her work with four-time Grammy-winning composer Laura Karpman produced a thrilling multimedia theater piece, *Ask Your Mama!,* featuring the poetry of Langston Hughes, which had its premiere at Carnegie Hall in March of 2009. The Jessye Norman School for the Arts in her hometown of Augusta, Georgia, is a tuition-free arts program for talented middle school students. She is the recipient of many accolades and awards, including five Grammys and a National Medal of the Arts.

Rosie O'Donnell is one of our most beloved performers. She has appeared in such films as *A League of Their Own* and *Sleepless in Seattle.* During her six years on *The Rosie O'Donnell Show,* she wrote her first book—a memoir called *Find Me.* As a tireless crusader for children, she established the For All Kids Foundation and Rosie's Broadway Kids. Today she hosts a daily Sirius radio show, Rosie Radio, and is a celebrity blogger, writing in her own unique style, on her popular Rosie.com website.

Dr. Mehmet Oz, host of *The Dr. Oz Show,* gained national media acclaim as a featured health expert on *The Oprah Winfrey Show* for over five seasons. He is vice-chair and professor of surgery at Columbia University and directs the Cardiovascular Institute and Complementary Medicine Program at New York–Presbyterian Hospital. In addition to belonging to every major professional society for heart surgeons, Dr. Oz is also the author of five *New York Times* bestsellers including *YOU: The Owner's Manual; YOU: The Smart Patient; YOU: On a Diet; YOU: Staying Young; YOU: Being Beautiful,* as well as the award-winning *Healing from the Heart.*

General Colin L. Powell served as the sixty-fifth US Secretary of State from January 2001 to January 2005. He served thirty-five years in the US Army, rising to the rank of four-star general, and from 1989 to 1993, he served as the twelfth Chairman of the Joint Chiefs of Staff. He also served as the National Security Advisor to President Ronald Reagan. General Powell is the author of his best-selling autobiography, *My American Journey.* General Powell is the founder of the Colin Powell Center for Policy Studies at his alma mater, the City College of New York.

Tony Randall was an American actor. Over his long career, Randall was nominated for five Golden Globe Awards and two Emmys, winning one Emmy in 1975 for his work on the sitcom *The Odd Couple.* He was the founder of the National Actors Theatre in New York City and starred in many plays, popular movies, and television shows. Randall died in 2004.

Christopher Reeve was an actor, director, and activist. From his first appearance at the Williamstown Theatre Festival at the age of fifteen, Reeve established a reputation as one of the country's leading actors. However, ever since he was paralyzed in an equestrian competition in 1995, Reeve not only put a human face on spinal cord injury, but he motivated neuroscientists around the world to conquer the most complex diseases of the brain and central nervous system. Christopher Reeve died in 2004 of heart failure.

Leonard Riggio is the chairman of Barnes & Noble Inc., a Fortune 500 company, which is the world's largest bookseller. In addition, he is the chairman and principal shareholder of several privately held companies, including Barnes & Noble College Booksellers, serving more than five hundred colleges and universities across America. He is also the founder and largest shareholder of GameStop, a Fortune 500 company, which operates five thousand video game stores worldwide. In all, the enterprises in which he is involved employ almost one hundred thousand people.

Chita Rivera, an accomplished and versatile actress, singer, and dancer, has won two Tony Awards as Best Leading Actress in a Musical and received seven additional Tony nominations. She recently starred in the Broadway and touring productions of *The Dancer's Life*, a dazzling new musical celebrating her spectacular career, written by Terence McNally and directed by Graciela Daniele. Rivera was awarded the Presidential Medal of Freedom by President Barack Obama on August 12, 2009. She received the coveted Kennedy Center Honor in Washington, DC, in December 2002; she is the first Hispanic ever chosen to receive this award.

Robin Roberts is anchor of ABC's *Good Morning America*. Under her leadership, the broadcast has won three consecutive Emmy Awards for Outstanding Morning Program. In 2008, Roberts' book, *From the Heart: 7 Rules to Live By*, was updated with an additional chapter on her battle with breast cancer. Her courageous and public battle has been recognized with awards and honors from organizations around the country, including The Susan G. Komen Foundation, The Congressional Families Cancer Prevention Program, and the nonprofit organization Gilda's Club.

Al Roker has built a unique place in television history as a host and weatherman on NBC's *Today* show. Each morning, this nine-time Emmy winner conducts interviews with celebrities, newsmakers, and regular people from around the world and a wide variety of segments on every imaginable subject. He is the host of many major NBC network specials, such as coverage of the Macy's Thanksgiving Day Parade, the Christmas tree lighting at Rockefeller Center, and the Rose Bowl Parade. He is also a best-selling author with four acclaimed books to his credit, including *Don't Make Me Stop This Car*, *Al Roker's Big Bad Book of Barbecue*, and *Big Shoes: In Celebration of Dads and Fatherhood*.

Tim Russert was moderator of *Meet the Press* and Washington bureau chief for NBC News. His two books, *Big Russ and Me* and *Wisdom of Our Fathers*, were number one *New York Times* bestsellers. From 1983 to 1984, he served as counselor to Governor Mario M. Cuomo of New York. Russert died in 2008.

Diane Sawyer is anchor of ABC's flagship *World News* broadcast. She is also the network's principal anchor for breaking news, election coverage, and special events. Sawyer is one of the most respected journalists in the world. Her primetime documentaries have won critical acclaim for shedding light on difficult and previously underreported topics. Sawyer's reporting has been recognized with numerous awards, including duPonts, Emmys, and Peabodys. In 1997, she was inducted into the Television Academy of Hall of Fame. A native of Glasgow, Kentucky, and raised in Louisville, Sawyer received a BA from Wellesley College.

Alan Schwartz is the executive chairman of Guggenheim Partners, which is a global, independent and privately held financial services firm. Mr. Schwartz is the former chief executive officer of The Bear Stearns Companies. During his career with Bear Stearns, he served as president and chief operating officer, as executive vice president and co-head of investment banking, and in other financial management positions. He previously worked in various capacities with Wertheim & Company and R. W. Pressprich & Company. He earned a BA in management science from Duke in 1972. He is member of the Duke Board of Trustees since 2005, has served as chairman of the Fuqua School of Business Board of Visitors and as a member of the

Athletic Advisory Board. Mr. Schwartz is a member of the boards of the Robin Hood Foundation, St. Vincent's Services, Marvin and Palmer, MENTOR: The National Mentoring Partnership, American Foundation for AIDS Research, and NYU Medical Center.

Martin Sheen is an award-winning journeyman actor and peace activist. For television, he is best known for his role as President Josiah Bartlet on *The West Wing*. Feature films include *Apocalypse Now, The Departed, Gandhi, Bobby,* and *Catch Me If You Can.*

Michael Strahan, Super Bowl Champion and *Fox NFL Sunday* cohost, retired from the NFL in 2007 after completing his fifteenth season with the New York Giants and leading the team to their dramatic Super Bowl victory over the previously unbeaten New England Patriots. Strahan is dedicated to many charitable works, donating hours and goodwill to numerous charities in the New York metropolitan area.

Joe Torre is a New York icon and one of baseball's most popular personalities. Torre is most famous for his successful career as manager of the New York Yankees. In 1996, Torre led the New York Yankees to their first World Series win since 1978. He went on to lead the Yankees to three straight World Series titles in 1998, 1999, and 2000. A former Major League Baseball player, Torre is also the coauthor of two books and a sought-after public speaker.

Stanley Tucci has appeared in over fifty films and countless television shows. He has also appeared in over a dozen plays, on and off Broadway. In the past few years he has appeared in films such as *Julie & Julia, The Devil Wears Prada, The Terminal, Road to Perdition,* and *The Lovely Bones,* for which he earned his first Academy Award nomination along with Golden Globe, BAFTA, SAG, and Broadcast Film Critics nominations. He is also a writer, director, and producer.

Meredith Vieira joined NBC's *Today* show as coanchor in 2006. She also serves as host of *Who Wants to Be a Millionaire,* for which she won a Daytime Emmy Award in August 2009. Prior to that, Vieira had been moderator of ABC's *The View* since the show's inception in 1997.

Early on, Vieira spent more than a decade at CBS News, where she garnered five Emmy Awards at *60 Minutes* and *West 57th.* Heavily involved with numerous philanthropic organizations, Vieira received the Safe Horizon Champion Award and the Woman of the Year Award from City of Hope. She has also been honored by the Anti-Defamation League.

Eli Wallach is one of Hollywood's finest character and method actors. He has been in demand for over fifty years on stage and screen. In 2005, Wallach released his autobiography, *The Good, The Bad, and Me: In My Anecdotage,* a wonderfully enjoyable read from one of the screen's most inventive and enduring actors.

Alice Waters, chef, author, and proprietor of Chez Panisse Restaurant in Berkeley, California, pioneered a culinary philosophy based on using only the freshest organic products, picked in season. Waters' commitment to education led to the creation of the Edible Schoolyard, a one-acre garden and adjacent kitchen classroom at Berkeley's Martin Luther King Jr. Middle School. Waters is vice president of Slow Food International, a nonprofit organization that promotes and celebrates local, artisanal food traditions. She is also the author of eight books.

Jamie Wyeth is a third-generation artist who lives and paints in Chadds Ford, Pennsylvania, and Tenants Harbor, Maine. Wyeth has had countless gallery exhibitions of his work and has served as a council member of the National Endowment for the Arts.

Fareed Zakaria is the host of CNN's flagship international affairs program, *Fareed Zakaria GPS,* an editor-at-large for *Time,* a *Washington Post* columnist, and a *New York Times* best-selling author. He was described in 1999 by *Esquire* as "the most influential foreign policy adviser of his generation." In 2007, *Foreign Policy* and *Prospect* magazines named him one of the one hundred leading public intellectuals in the world. Dr. Zakaria received a BA from Yale College and a PhD from Harvard University. He lives in New York City with his wife, son, and two daughters.